The Lost Detective

BY THE SAME AUTHOR

Dark Harbor: The War for the New York Waterfront
The Total Sports Illustrated Book of Boxing
(coeditor, with W. C. Heinz)

The Lost Detective

Becoming Dashiell Hammett

Nathan Ward

B L O O M S B U R Y

NEW YORK · LONDON · OXFORD · NEW DELHI · SYDNEY

Bloomsbury USA
An imprint of Bloomsbury Publishing Plc

1385 Broadway   50 Bedford Square
New York   London
NY 10018   WC1B 3DP
USA   UK

www.bloomsbury.com

BLOOMSBURY and the Diana logo are trademarks of Bloomsbury Publishing Plc

First published 2015

© Nathan Ward, 2015

All rights reserved. No part of this publication may be reproduced or transmitted in
any form or by any means, electronic or mechanical, including photocopying,
recording, or any information storage or retrieval system, without prior permission
in writing from the publishers.

No responsibility for loss caused to any individual or organization acting on or
refraining from action as a result of the material in this publication can be accepted
by Bloomsbury or the author.

ISBN: HB: 978-0-80277-640-2
          ePub: 978-1-63286-277-8

LIBRARY OF CONGRESS CATALOGING-IN-PUBLICATION DATA

Ward, Nathan, 1963–
The lost detective : becoming Dashiell Hammett / Nathan Ward.
pages cm
Includes bibliographical references and index.
ISBN 978-0-8027-7640-2 (hardback) / 978-1-63286-277-8 (ePub)
1. Hammett, Dashiell, 1894-1961.   2. Authors, American—20th century—
Biography.   3. Detective and mystery stories, American—History and criticism.
I. Title.   II. Title: Becoming Dashiell Hammett.
PS3515.A4347Z92 2015
813'.52—dc23
[B]
2015016402

2 4 6 8 10 9 7 5 3 1

Typeset by RefineCatch Limited, Bungay, Suffolk
Printed and bound in the U.S.A. by Thomson-Shore Inc., Dexter, Michigan

To find out more about our authors and books visit www.bloomsbury.com. Here
you will find extracts, author interviews, details of forthcoming events and the
option to sign up for our newsletters.

Bloomsbury books may be purchased for business or promotional use. For
information on bulk purchases please contact Macmillan Corporate and Premium
Sales Department at specialmarkets@macmillan.com.

For Katie, as ever.
And for the Calhouns,
who showed me the West.

CONTENTS

[W]hatever the intrinsic moral life or character of the detective may be, his art is a devilish one, and civilization is responsible for it.

—OFFICER GEORGE S. MCWATTERS,
KNOTS UNTIED (1871)

The cheaper the crook, the gaudier the patter.

—SAM SPADE IN *THE MALTESE FALCON* (1930)

I've testified before juries all the way from the city of Washington to the state of Washington, and I've never seen one yet that wasn't anxious to believe that a private detective is a double-crossing specialist who goes around with a cold deck in one pocket, a complete forger's outfit in another, and who counts that day lost in which he railroads no innocent to the hoosegow.

—DASHIELL HAMMETT, "ZIGZAGS OF
TREACHERY" (1924)

Prelude

SCARS

At a cocktail party in Manhattan in late January 1939, a gaunt, elegant man in a double-breasted suit sat down and laid one of his long pale hands before a fortune-teller. The man was quiet and watchful, his face handsome in a lean and angular way, his age blurred a bit by his grizzled mustache and pompadour gone prematurely white. He might have cradled a drink with one hand while he offered the palm of the other for interpreting, from his tapering fingers to the intersection of his fate and heart lines.

Had the fortune-teller examined both his hands, she might have noticed clues that he hadn't always lived so well. Down at the fleshy part of his left palm, near the curved base of his thumb, was the remaining tip of a knifepoint lodged there during a time in his life when he didn't dress so beautifully or live at the Plaza. Whether or not he told the reader his profession was largely unnecessary: he was widely recognized from the cover of his last book, a popular novel that had inspired three movies in four years.

Assembling her available evidence, the reader offered her predictions for the coming decade, which the man happily passed on in a letter to his older daughter:

I . . . was told that the most successful years of my life would be from 1941 to 1948, that most of my real troubles were behind me, that I was going to make a lot of money out of two entirely different lines of work, plus a sideline, and that I'll have most luck with women born in December. So I'd be sitting pretty if I could make myself believe in palmistry, and if I knew any women born in December![1]

In fact, while he would continue to have luck with all sorts of women, some even born in December, on the other front his best years were well behind him. Ahead were war and a grateful return to the army, a prison term and blacklisting, hard drinking, illness, and poverty. He would never finish another book, though he would start a number of them, but the lasting mystery of Dashiell Hammett was not why he stopped writing, since he hadn't. It was how he came to the writing life at all.

★ ★ ★

SCARS HAD MADE him credible. When they were young, Hammett used to show his daughters the marks of his old trade—let them see the cuts on his legs or feel the dent in his skull where he'd once been knocked by a brick. His old wounds summoned up stories from a romantic past: he told some people that the brick had come from an angry striker while he was doing anti-union work for Pinkerton's, but both Hammett girls remembered another version, more typical of their father for its mingling of self-mockery with suspense. He was, after all, a man whose roof perch had once collapsed while on stakeout and who had fallen from a taxicab during a city chase.

"One of my earliest memories is of getting to feel the dent in his head from being hit by a brick when he bungled a tailing job," remembered his younger daughter, Jo Hammett, "and he let me see the knife tip embedded in the palm of his hand."*[2] Her sister, Mary, told the private detective and historian David Fechheimer, "You could feel it in later years. There was a dent in the back of his head like the corner of a brick."[3]

It might have been thrown by an angry striker, as Hammett occasionally claimed, or have been dropped on him by a shadow subject who surprised him in San Francisco, as reported by his wife, who watched him suffer for days afterward in a chair. In the thirties, he gave another account of being wounded in the course of arresting a "gang of negroes" accused of stealing dynamite in Baltimore during the war. "When I got inside this house men were being knocked around in fine shape. In the excitement I had a feeling something was wrong but I could not figure out what it was till I happened to look down and saw this Negro whittling away at my leg."[4] In the end, there was the dent and the scars and the gift for storytelling, his conversation hinting at a detecting career as colorful as it was peripatetic: the jewel thief nicknamed the Midget Bandit, in Stockton, California; the swindler in Seattle; the forger he trapped in Pasco, Washington; the imposing railroad worker he tricked into custody in Montana; and the Indian he arrested for murder in Arizona.

How did he get from detective to writer? Hammett never answered satisfactorily. He was a Pinkerton, then he was very

---

* When recently asked to recall on which hand she remembered seeing her father's famous knifepoint scar, Jo Hammett answered through her daughter Julie Rivett that she was pretty sure it was his left hand. This suggests he got the wound shielding himself against a knife blow with his nondominant hand.

sick, then he was peddling stories to magazines, with apparently little more ambition than that, at least at the beginning. "Maybe man-hunting isn't the nicest trade in the world," says the skinny, ungentlemanly operative in Hammett's first detective story, "The Road Home," "but it's all the trade I've got."[5] It was the trade Samuel Dashiell Hammett knew best at age twenty-eight when his bad lungs forced him to give it up.

Three years after he left Pinkerton's, on a late-summer day in 1925, Josephine Dolan Hammett took a photograph of her husband sitting in the sun up on the roof of their apartment building, on Eddy Street in San Francisco: a young man wearing a tweed cap and sweater-vest, looking confident and wickedly thin, strikes a match across the sole of his shoe to light a gauzy cigarette he has rolled himself, like someone he might have invented downstairs at his writing table. The picture shows a graying young father who writes with growing poise about the rough types and places he used to know. By the mid-1920s, Hammett's detective experiences were like a set of tools he rummaged through and sharpened as needed for his craft.

"Shadowing is the easiest of detective work," he boasted as an ex-Pinkerton, "except, perhaps, to an extremely nervous man. You simply saunter along somewhere within sight of your subject; and, barring bad breaks, the only thing that can make you lose him is overanxiety on your own part."[6] The literary people with whom he shared such wisdom ate it up.

Hammett might never have written anything but love poetry and ad copy had he not first taken the rough detour into detective work. It gave him "authority," he explained later, as well as a subject, enabling him to lecture his fellow crime writers in book reviews about the difference between a revolver and an automatic, for instance, or on how counterfeiting schemes really worked, what it felt like to be stabbed or clubbed unconscious, or where to find the best fingerprints. "It would be silly to insist that nobody who has not been a detective should write detective stories,"[7] he declared, but he didn't seem to think it was all that silly if it sifted out the lazier writers.

At the time he started sending out stories in the early 1920s, Hammett was not alone in looking at American urban life in a new, unsparing way, but among writers he was a rarity in having such experience with criminals and their gaudy talk. "I can do better than that," he'd said to his wife early on after reading pulp magazines in the San Francisco Public Library, and it turned out that he could. That summer of 1925, when he took the portrait on the roof, his health was bad, but he nevertheless continued publishing his series of increasingly popular crime stories featuring a nameless operative for the fictional Continental Detective Agency, Op Number 7. If you read his Op stories in order, you can watch a sickly ex-detective in his late twenties, with an eighth-grade education, gradually, improbably, teach himself to write, mentored by criminologists, historians, and novelists he brought home from what he called his "university," the public library.

Hammett lost himself in creating these dark adventures, and while his stories brought in extra money, they also allowed him to keep playing at the investigating he could no longer physically carry out himself:

I climbed Telegraph Hill to give the house the up-and-down.
It was a large house—a big frame house painted egg-yellow. It

hung dizzily on a shoulder of the hill, a shoulder that was
sharp where rock had been quarried away. The house seemed
about to go skiing down on the roofs far below.[8]

What he wrote was at odds with the largely English tradi-
tion of detective fiction, a gentlemanly deductive exercise in
which the reader followed an aloof inspector to the crime's
brilliant solution, often set at an English country estate. The
Pinkertons had taught him an opposite lesson: that most crimes
were actually solved by detectives who were observant and
who circulated among the grifters, gangsters, forgers, and hop
heads. "A private detective does not want to be an erudite
solver of riddles," Hammett explained; "he wants to be a hard
and shifty fellow, able to take care of himself in any situation,
able to get the best of anybody he comes in contact with,
whether criminal, innocent by-stander or client."[9]

He dispensed with the investigator's chess game, paring
down to a more American style that was both deft and tough:

> On Spade's desk a limp cigarette smoldered in a brass tray
> filled with the remains of limp cigarettes. Ragged grey
> flakes of cigarette-ash dotted the yellow top of the desk
> and the green blotter and the papers that were there. A buff-
> curtained window, eight or ten inches open, let in from the
> court a current of air faintly scented with ammonia. The
> ashes on the desk twitched and crawled in the current.[10]

These are the observations of an Ashcan painter or a detective
poet, a kind of cinematic writing that had yet even to appear on
a screen in the late twenties. It is the voice of a hard and shifty

fellow. When professors argue about who invented the stripped-down American prose of the twentieth century—Hemingway? Stein? Sherwood Anderson? Hammett?—the battle is often confined to the realm of published literature, of who read what and when they read it. But if anything taught Hammett to write pithily and with appreciation for the language of street characters it was not discovering an early Hemingway story in the *Transatlantic Review*, but doing his scores of operative reports for the Pinkerton National Detective Agency.

Imagine a tall, lean young man in a neat, plain suit, reddish temples showing beneath his soft hat, waiting skinnily against a wall like an unused rake; or timing his long stride to stay nestled among the moving pack of strangers along a downtown sidewalk. Picture him settling behind his sports page aboard a train, paid to watch the dining car for signs of petty thieving, or studying the bow-tied passenger on the aisle inherited from a brother Pinkerton going off watch.

Being an operative gave Hammett work as he relocated across the country (Baltimore, Spokane, Seattle, San Francisco), and since the ops routinely had their reports edited or rewritten by supervisors for their Pinkerton clients, the experience made up a kind of literary training, just as Hammett later insisted.

How could the poised creator of *The Maltese Falcon* or *Red Harvest* have come to a writing career so late, seemingly without the customary years of practice and ambition? One answer lies in the hundreds of operative reports in boxes at the Pinkerton archives in the Library of Congress in Washington, D.C. Sadly, Hammett's own dispatches are not among them, but those of his contemporaries in the Agency show how much of his approach was encouraged by their general training: the habits of observation, the light touch and nonjudgment while writing studiously about lowlifes. He just took it further.

His Continental Op stories clearly evolved from the form of these Pinkerton reports, which is not to say any of his colleagues could have written his stories or books, but that the seasoning he received on the job was crucial to what he later became. Among the better Pinkerton writers there was in-house competitive name-dropping of street monikers, to show they were "assimilating" with the right crooks, as the founder, Allan Pinkerton, had insisted they do.

Hammett claimed to have learned about writing at the agency, where he clearly acquired some of his craft reading dozens of memos such as this one (from 1901) by Assistant Superintendent Beutler of the New York office, whose stable of informants might have held their own in any of Hammett's stories:

> To-night, on my return from the race track, I met Informant Birdstone in Engel's Chop house, where we had supper together. He stated that several bands of pickpockets were now being got together for the purpose of following President McKinley on his jaunting trip . . . The crooks are to meet in the vicinity of Houston, Tex. One band is headed by "Bull" Hurley, Charlie Hess, "Big Eddie" Fritz and Pete Raymond, a California pickpocket. Another by John Lester, Dyke and Joe Pryor, alias "Walking Joe," "Hob nail" Reilly, Parkinson, a Chicago pickpocket, and Billy Seymour.[11]

It's not a huge stretch to imagine Hob Nail Reilly or Walking Joe Pryor sharing a jail cell a few years later with any of the gang summoned for the epic bank job in Hammett's *The Big Knockover*: Toby the Lugs, Fat Boy Clarke, Alphabet Shorty McCoy, the type of men a sharp Pinkerton would have cultivated for his files.

Just as the *Kansas City Star* (with its famous style sheet requiring short sentences and vigorous English) helped shape the prose of the young Ernest Hemingway, out of the scores of men trained as Pinkertons, one emerged from the Agency able to make something entirely new from his experiences. "Detecting has its high spots," Hammett recalled in the twenties, "but the run of the work is the most monotonous that any one could imagine. The very things that can be made to sound the most exciting in the telling are in the doing usually the most dully tiresome." His deeper skills lay in that telling.

Over a five-year run, Hammett took command of the crime writing field, publishing the novels *Red Harvest*, *The Dain Curse*, *The Maltese Falcon*, and *The Glass Key* between 1929 and 1931, and adding *The Thin Man* in 1934. By the early thirties, he was a poor man turned suddenly flush, his fortunes risen even as the country slid into depression; he had gone to New York with a woman not his wife, the writer Nell Martin, kept a car and a chauffeur and spent well beyond his considerable means at fancy hotels on both coasts, sending postcards and matchbooks to his daughters from the lobbies of his new life, which often had a flamboyant unreality like the movies.

Hammett liked to embellish his old Pinkerton career, especially when flogging new projects in newspaper interviews. Had the California cable car robbery, a bold noontime holdup of company payroll on a moving cable car, been his final case, or was it the gold theft aboard the steamer SS *Sonoma*? Did he work for the defense on the first rape and manslaughter trial of the comedian Fatty Arbuckle in 1921, or was he already too sick? (He would give a convincing description of spotting Arbuckle in a San Francisco hotel lobby: "His eyes were the eyes of a man who expected to be seen as a monster but was not yet inured to it.")

Sometimes it was the *Sonoma* case that had finished Hammett's detective career; other times, the trapping of "Gloomy Gus" Schaefer for robbery, complete with a tale of Hammett's riding down a collapsing porch while on stakeout. Had he really decided there was "more fun in writing about manhunting than in that hunting," as he remembered it in 1924, or had his bad lungs forced his decision? "[B]eing a professional busy-body requires more energy, more dogged patience, than you'd suppose," he said five years later. "There never was anything lacking in the matter of my curiosity."[12]

One story he relished telling, about being offered five thousand dollars to kill an organizer for the International Workers of the World named Frank Little during a miners' strike in 1917, shocked most people he knew since it ran so afoul of his later radical beliefs. When Hammett claimed he had once turned down a bribe to kill the Wobbly agitator (as IWW members were known), his daughter Mary recalled in 1975, "It was a shock when I heard about it and I said, 'You mean you were working for Pinkerton against the IWW?' And he said, 'That's right.'"[13] He didn't care "if his clients were bums," Mary added. "He was strictly out to do his job." HE DIDN'T CARE IF HIS CLIENTS WERE BUMS. HE WAS STRICTLY OUT TO DO HIS JOB would make a nice epitaph for his most famous creation, Sam Spade.

By the time the detectives he'd invented had their own renown, the one Hammett had been himself was cloudy, cloaked in his own disguising, and unacknowledged by the Pinkerton agency that had supposedly trained him in the devilish arts. Yet all his investigators were extensions in one direction or another of the one he had been himself: the gritty little company man of the Op stories who lives for the dogged joys of sleuthing; the handsome, wolfish PI Sam Spade, who does whatever he must for his client (a "dream man," Hammett wrote, "what most of the private detectives I worked with would like to have been"); the tall, tubercular fixer on an unlucky gambling streak, Ned Beaumont, battling in a town very like Hammett's native Baltimore; and finally, the glib and cynical Nick Charles, the ex-detective from San Francisco whose life is one long charmed bender.

Hammett was not a diarist, and he pitched most of his letters as he moved around. His transformation from working detective to writer was in part a function of his sickly health, and his U.S. Army medical file tells the biography of his illness—the vagaries of his weight and lung capacity and official judgments of his disability from the time of his discharge in 1919. With tuberculosis he was slowly incapacitated out of conventional employment, especially the detective work he'd largely enjoyed. Still needing money for his family, but often too sick to leave his apartment, he took a stab at writing.

Part I

THE CHEAPER THE CROOK

[The detective] must appear the careless, ordinary individual, particularly to those upon whom he is to operate. Assimilating, as far as possible, with the individuals who are destined to feel the force of his authority, and by appearing to know but little, acquire all the information possible to gather from every conceivable source.

—ALLAN PINKERTON, *THIRTY YEARS A DETECTIVE* (1884)

A good detective has to be brave, vigorous, damnably clever, tireless—altogether a real person! His is an extraordinarily complicated mechanism.

—DASHIELL HAMMETT, 1929

I had started out with the big agency to see the world and learn human nature.

—CHARLIE SIRINGO, *A COWBOY DETECTIVE*

Chapter I

THE DEVILISH ART

BALTIMORE, 1915

EVEN IF HE had finished alongside his high school class-mates at Baltimore Polytechnic Institute, it is difficult to imagine Samuel D. Hammett among the self-possessed upper-classmen pictured in the school's yearbooks, old-looking boys in dark suits with class pages touting their skills in metalwork and German translation. Instead, he left school at age fourteen to help his family, and over the five and a half years since then, he had tried on a variety of professions and laid all of them aside: office messenger for the B&O railroad, paperboy, dock-worker, nail machine operator, "very junior" advertising clerk, timekeeper in a cannery, salesman for his father's hapless seafood business. He was often let go "most amiably," he recalled.

The family had lived in both Philadelphia and Baltimore since Sam's birth on May 27, 1894, at the Hammett tobacco farm, Hopewell and Aim, in St. Mary's County, Maryland; born, as he put it, between the Potomac and Patuxent Rivers. Sam was named for his paternal grandfather, Samuel Biscoe Hammett Jr., who, after the death of his first wife in the 1880s, had married a much younger woman named Lucy with whom he started a second family almost contemporaneous with the arrival of his grandchildren. All of them crowded into the three-story farmhouse. After losing a bitterly fought county election, young Sam's father, Richard Thomas Hammett, sought a fresh start by moving his own family, a wife and three young children, briefly to Philadelphia. He experienced disappointments in that city, too, and in 1901 he moved the family again, this time to Baltimore and the row house rented by his wife's mother at 212 North Stricker Street, near Franklin Square. He had gone from the house of his father to that of his wife's mother, with brief failures in between.

Though Richard's ambitions tended more toward politics, his social skills and temperament did not; he took a job as a streetcar conductor, and the Hammett children entered Public School Number 72. As a city boy, young Sam Hammett could cite his country roots, and when he returned on summer visits to his grandfather's farm, he could just as rightly put on citified airs. The family would move twice more around Baltimore, only to return to the mother-in-law's when Richard's political and business schemes fell through. This would be Sam's home until he was in his twenties.

From boyhood, Hammett was an incorrigible reader and prowler of public libraries whose tastes ran from swash-bucklers and dime Westerns to edifying works of European philosophy and manuals of technical expertise. It was a habit that nourished him early on and sustained him through his later illnesses flat on his back. While a boy, his late-night reading sessions often left him difficult to rouse in the morning, complained his mother, Annie Bond Hammett, a small, frail, yet forthright woman known as Lady, who supported his curiosity and certainly encouraged his confidence. The narrator of Hammett's autobiographical fragment, *Tulip*, remembers this about his mother:

> She never gave me but two pieces of advice and they were both good. "Never go out in a boat without oars, son," she said, "even if it's the Queen Mary; and don't waste your time on women who can't cook because they're not likely to be much fun in the other rooms either."

It was probably Annie Hammett who met the census taker at the door of their row house in Philadelphia in 1900, since it was recorded that 2942 Poplar Street was then home to three children: Reba, Richard, and a six-year-old middle child, "Dashell." Hammett's evolution from Sam to Dashiell is not a straight line, but his mother certainly called him Dashiell (Da-SHEEL) as a boy, a name he later put on his stories and books and, ultimately, came to be called by almost everyone.* Hammett seems to have had a strong and comfortable relationship with his mother and his older sister, Reba, and would get on more easily with women

---

* His wife, Josephine Dolan Hammett, reported in 1975 that he was "always" called Sam until the success of the Op stories and novels in the late 1920s, when his new literary and Hollywood friends called him Dash. But his granddaughter Julie Rivett points out that he sometimes signed letters to his wife "D" or "Dash" (starting in 1928). Of course, that is only evidence that he had begun to use the name himself. But this census record suggests that he was called Dashiell, at least by his mother, as early as 1900. Employers, schoolmates, army chums, cousins, and his wife, though, knew him as Sam. Lillian Hellman came along during his famous Dash years.

throughout his life. According to his second cousin Jane Fish Yowaiski, later interviewed by Josiah Thompson, only Sam's mother could make him go to church.

No writing about Annie neglects to point out how she held herself a little above her husband's family, and not without reason. She proudly told her children about her own mother's people, who were originally French Huguenots called the De Schiells (pronounced Da-SHEEL, like Hammett's middle name within the family), a surname Americanized as "Dashiell." The family was at least as settled as the Hammetts, whose earliest ancestor in Maryland died in 1719. James Dashiell had arrived in the state in 1663, according to a family history, cropping the ears of his cattle in the fleur-de-lis pattern favored by his French grandmother. Sam's mother told him tales of the Old World De Schiells filled with chateaux and knights, passing along their rather unambitious family motto, "Ny Tost Ny Tard" ("Neither Soon nor Late").

Because Richard Hammett's family always needed money Annie Hammett worked private nursing jobs when possible, despite a chronic cough and weakness that otherwise kept her close to home. Hammett seems to have shared his mother's opinion that Richard Hammett was not worthy of her, or at least that he could have treated her much better: in addition to his failures as a breadwinner (as a manufacturer agent, then a clerk, salesman, and a conductor) Richard was something of a ladies' man who liked to dress sharp for his other women. Hammett's cousin Jane Yowaiski recalled Richard's visits to her family in the 1930s, looking like "the Governor of Maryland" and often driven by attractive younger women whom he'd introduce as his "friend."[1]

By the time he was twenty, Sam was a gangly and quiet young man with reddish hair who liked to fish and hunt and drink and who vastly preferred the company of women and books to what he'd seen of the working world. Like the father he quarreled with, Sam was a bit of a loafer and aspiring ladies' man. (Early that same year, 1915, he caught his first dose of gonorrhea, possibly from a woman he had met while working near the train yards. It would not be his last case of the clap.) Still living with his parents, he increasingly turned up late to work, if not also hungover from his growing nightlife.

"I became the unsatisfactory and unsatisfied employee of various railroads, stock brokers, machine manufacturers, canners, and the like," he remembered. "Usually I was fired."[2] According to Hammett, his boss at the B&O Railroad office attempted to cut him loose after a week of late arrivals, then relented when he refused to lie and promise to do better, delaying the inevitable.

At twenty his most recent positions had been with the Baltimore brokerage house Poe & Davies, where his lateness and sloppiness with sums got him fired, and as a dockworker, where "I made the grade but then it became too strenuous."[3] He passed some idle weeks before something else caught his eye in the newspaper, an "enigmatic want-ad" seeking capable young men with a range of experience like his own who were fond of travel. Although the exact newspaper message has never been identified, according to one former employee from this era, the company's blind recruitment ads were pretty much of a piece:

WANTED—A bright, experienced salesman to handle good line; salary and commission. Excellent opportunity for right man to connect with first-class house.[4]

Hammett mailed in his reply, then was called downtown to interview in a suite at the Continental Trust Company building on Baltimore Street, an office tower whose sixteen floors were guarded by small stone falcons. The position, it turned out, was not in either sales or insurance but something with the Baltimore office of the Pinkerton National Detective Agency. "The fortunes of job-hunting not guided by definite vocational training had taken him into the employ of a private detective agency," Hammett wrote of another detective in "The Hunter."

Pinkerton's was looking for detectives, or "general operatives," as the agency preferred, and by advertising instead for other professions the company maintained its secrecy. Many of the skills of salespeople, for instance, served well in operative work, especially the ability to quickly size up a stranger without raising suspicion, but the murky ads were also used to recruit for Pinkerton's strikebreaking efforts. Hammett would work at both.

According to one former Pinkerton, a good general operative was a man "who can be relied upon to do the right thing, even in the absence of instructions from the executive department, and who will at all times act in a cool, discreet and level-headed manner."[5] A hoarder of quirky knowledge from his wide reading, Hammett must also have impressed his interviewer as cool, discreet and level-headed, because he was hired as a Pinkerton clerk, and within months was an agency operative. Now twenty-one, he had lucked into hard, unpredictable work that peculiarly suited him with the country's oldest and largest detective agency. "The eye of the detective must never sleep," Allan Pinkerton wrote, and Hammett soon discovered that operatives were expected to work every day of the week, if needed. The company's symbol, an unblinking eye above the motto "We Never Sleep," had given rise to a popular term its founder disliked: *private eye.*

An operative's life took him everywhere and nowhere, and by following the basic laws for shadowing, he could go unnoticed for hours or even days at a time. "Keep behind your subject as much as possible," Hammett later summed up tailing for his civilian public, "never try to hide from him; act in a natural manner no matter what happens; and never meet his eye."[6]

For a young man whose formal instruction had ended only months into high school, the Pinkerton Agency offered a unique education, which he continued to supplement at public libraries. There is no indication he wanted to write as early as 1915, but the agency helped form the writer he became as surely as working at a newspaper might have. A veteran operative recalled joining Pinkerton's "to see the world and learn human nature."[7]

Allan Pinkerton was long gone by the time Hammett joined the company, although his imprint was everywhere. The Scottish immigrant had gradually transformed himself, through a job he invented, into the leader of a kind of national police force that could chase criminals unhindered by state or county lines. In his many books (ghostwritten and otherwise) he sketched a clear picture of his dogged ideal investigator:

> The profession of the detective is, at once, an honorable and highly useful one. For practical benefits few professions excel it. He is an officer of justice, and must himself be pure and above reproach . . . The great essential is to prevent his identity from becoming known, even among his associates of respectable character, and when he fails to do this; when the nature of his calling is discovered and made known his

usefulness to the profession is at an end, and failure certain
and inevitable is the result.[8]

Pinkerton took his own circuitous path to sleuthing. He was
born in Glasgow, Scotland, in 1819, and while working as a
barrel maker, he became involved in the Scottish Chartist labor
movement (from which he later borrowed the term *operative*),
before trouble with the police over his activism led him to
emigrate with his wife in 1842. After several false starts together,
the couple settled in the village of Dundee, Illinois, northwest of
Chicago, where they built a small house and Pinkerton opened
a reasonably profitable business supplying barrels to the farmers
of the region. Pinkerton differed from a number of his neighbors in that he was a teetotaler and an abolitionist; in addition to
sheltering his growing young family, Pinkerton's modest house
was home to runaways traveling North to freedom.

The first American detective agency grew out of the suspicions of a young man searching for wood. To cut his material
costs, Pinkerton would hunt for timber to make his barrel
staves, poling his barge along the nearby Fox River and harvest-
ing from unclaimed stands of trees along the route. He was
several miles upriver, near the town of Algonquin, Illinois,
in June 1846, when he discovered something that would push
his cooper's life off course. A small island in the middle of
the river belonged to no one, and Pinkerton set to work one
morning felling and cutting up what he needed when he
spotted a blackened patch of ground, proof of an earlier camp-
fire, and other signs of repeated visits by strangers. The fire
seemed suspect. "There was no picnicking in those days, people
had more serious matters to attend to and it required no great

keenness to conclude that no honest men were in the habit of occupying the place."⁹

Pinkerton visited the island several times to find other hints of secret meetings. Then, while watching it one night, he saw a group of men land and gather conspiratorially around a fire. He returned once more, bringing the sheriff and a posse, who arrested a group of counterfeiters caught with their tools and "a bag of bogus dimes." After this triumph, on what came to be called Bogus Island, Pinkerton was solicited by local businessmen for his help cracking another counterfeiting gang. He declined, citing his cooperage business, before his sense of justice got the better of him and he accepted his first paid job of sleuthing.

Pinkerton's activism had got him chased to America in the first place, and running for county sheriff on the Abolitionist ticket in 1847 brought to a head his conflict with the pastor of the local Dundee Baptist Church, who put him on trial for atheism and "selling ardent spirits." The slander led Pinkerton to accept a job as assistant sheriff of Cook County and move to Chicago, then a filthy but growing city of nearly thirty thousand people. There, sometime around 1850, he opened the country's first detective firm, the North-Western Police Agency, which evolved into Pinkerton's National Detective Agency.* He would popularize the use of rap sheets, rogues'

---

* The world's first private detective firm had been started in France, in 1833, by a former thief and police spy named François Eugene Vidocq, whose florid life inspired characters by Poe, Balzac, Hugo, Dumas, and Conan Doyle. Vidocq had earlier recruited many former criminal colleagues to establish the Parisian plainclothes security force La Sûreté in 1811.

galleries, mug shots, and fingerprints, and he hired the first female detectives decades before the City of New York had any.

Crimes were not solved by aloof geniuses, Pinkerton long contended, but by an operative being an observant student of human nature who guarded his identity as if his life depended on it, a knight who could pass as a rogue, "Assimilating, as far as possible, with the individuals who are destined to feel the force of his authority."[10]

The Pinkerton Agency grew in the years when many frontier towns had no municipal police force, while those that did have small ones still saw criminals escape over county lines. "The history of all places which have had a rapid growth is full of startling incidents of crime," Pinkerton explained, creating "opportunities for criminal deeds so numerous, as to sometimes create an epidemic of wrong-doing."[11] Such epidemics became Pinkerton's opportunity. In 1855 he had the good fortune to sign a contract to protect the Illinois Central Railroad, whose director, George McClellan, and company attorney, Abraham Lincoln, were men on the rise.

In 1861, Pinkerton uncovered a "Baltimore Plot" against the newly elected president; he spirited Lincoln by train safely through the heart of the conspiracy to his inaugural, and served for a time as his wartime intelligence chief. In a famous war photograph of Lincoln visiting a Union campsite, Pinkerton is right there, hiding in plain sight, identified by his alias "Major Allen," a stocky, glowering figure in a dark beard and bowler beside the elongated man in the top hat.

To the end of his life, Allan Pinkerton held to the methods roughed out in his first cases. In *The Model Town and the Detectives*, he recalled being visited by a man representing a group of Illinois merchants whose community was experiencing a wave of thefts. "I told him that I would undertake to clear the town of its active scoundrels, on condition that I should be allowed to work in my own way without interference by any one, and that my instructions be obeyed implicitly." Pinkerton scouted the town himself, under an assumed name and dressed as a farmer, before unleashing his undercover operatives into the saloons and boardinghouses.

Clearing the town of active scoundrels is what some Hammett heroes do, even if they don't always keep to Mr. Pinkerton's other rules of detecting. Pinkerton broke plenty of his own rules as well, when the case was important enough, the most egregious example being his war with the James gang in the 1870s. "I know that the James' and the Youngers are desperate men," Pinkerton wrote to his New York office, "and that when we meet it must be the death of one or both of us."[12]

After one of his detectives, J. W. Whicher, was abducted, tortured, and murdered point blank by the gang in 1874, a Pinkerton supervisor analyzed the agent's deadly error: "He was roughly dressed, but when he got there they must have noticed that he was a sharp, penetrating-looking fellow, and they probably took notice of his soft hands."[13] In fact, Operative Whicher's biggest mistake, beyond going in alone, had been to identify himself to the local sheriff, George E. Patton, a one-armed Confederate veteran and boyhood friend of the James boys, to whom he boasted of his plans to go undercover and infiltrate the gang.

"My blood is spilt, and they must repay," Pinkerton wrote his New York superintendent, George Bangs, and sent a contingent to the Missouri farmhouse of the Jameses' mother, whose weatherboarded windows prevented lawmen from getting a bead on possible targets inside. Bob and Jesse were not in the house—Jesse was in fact away on a kind of honeymoon in Nashville—but the Pinkertons' plan was to toss in a large incendiary device meant to light up the interior and smoke any of the gang from the building. Instead, it ended up in the fireplace and exploded, killing Frank and Jesse's nine-year-old half-brother with iron shrapnel and maiming their mother's right hand, which had to be amputated, adding fresh sympathy to the cause of the folkloric gang around the country. In this rare case, Pinkerton knew when he was licked and bitterly quit the hunt.*

In the years following his death in 1884, Allan Pinkerton's sons divided control of the agency into eastern and western headquarters, and increased the firm's protection work. With the Homestead steel strike of 1892, the Pinkertons had another disastrous public lesson, that serving openly as armed strikebreakers in labor violence could be riskier than more stealthy modes of detecting.

Their railroad contacts had led the company into the pursuit of outlaw gangs who robbed the express companies; following the company's success infiltrating the deadly society of the Molly Maguires in the Pennsylvania coalfields, the Pinkertons inserted nervy labor spies into union after union, reporting the

---

* Many accounts repeat the claim that Jesse's son (not half-bother) was killed by the Pinkerton blast; in fact, the outlaw was away in Nashville with his new bride, and his first son was born on New Year's Eve, 1875. The most accurate version is in Ron Hansen's beautifully faithful novel, *The Assassination of Jesse James by the Coward Robert Ford*.

inside strategies of strike committees directly to company executives, often daily. Certain individual detectives, such as the
Thiel Agency's "Operative 58A" (Edward L Zimmerman) or
the Pinkerton's Charlie Siringo became celebrated for their
undercover daring, even as the mining companies they risked
their lives in service of were reviled as "crushers of labor."

As a reader of detective and cowboy stories, Hammett would
have known the career of the "Cowboy Detective" Charlie
Siringo and his adventures "on mountain and plain, among
moonshiners, cattle thieves, tramps, dynamiters, and strong-
arm men." But Siringo's life as a detective also offered a caution
for any operative tempted to tell tales out of school. The year
Hammett started at the Agency, 1915, had been the year of
Siringo's second attempt to tell the story of his exciting two
decades with the Pinkertons. Born in Matagorda County,
Texas, Siringo was a working cowboy by age eleven, and while
living in Chicago as a young man, he witnessed the deadly
Haymarket Square bombing and riot in 1886, leaving him
wishing he were a detective "so as to ferret out the thrower of
the bomb and his backers." When he went to the Chicago
Pinkerton headquarters, he cited the lawman Pat Garrett, killer
of Billy the Kid, as a reference.

Siringo became part of the Pinkerton posse that chased
Butch Cassidy's Hole-in-the-Wall Gang, and he went undercover as a miner in an ore-stealing case in Aspen. Then, during
the Coeur d'Alene mining strikes in Idaho, he got himself
elected recording secretary of the gem miners' union before
being discovered as a spy. He escaped through the floorboards
of a building in Gem, Idaho, and crawled for some yards
beneath the wooden sidewalk, where an outraged mob was

waiting to kill him. In public, he was often picturesquely armed with his sidekick cane-sword and Colt. 45, and he served as bodyguard to his fellow Pinkerton detective William McParland when the latter investigated for the prosecution in the murder of the former Idaho governor Frank Steunenberg in 1905.

Siringo learned the limits of the Pinkertons' tolerance when he tried to publish his memoir, *Cowboy Detective* (1912). Although the book read like a recruitment manual for the detective's life, the Pinkerton family held up publication for two years, until Siringo had changed many crucial names, most especially that of the "world-famous" detective firm that employed him, substituting the fictional "Dickenson" Agency. In 1915, greatly soured by his treatment, he tried again with the vengeful *Two Evil Isms: Pinkertonism and Anarchism*. This time he told many stories too dark for the heroic first account, explaining how he was paid to vote five times in one day in a Colorado election, and why he had repeatedly refused promotions in what he called "the most corrupt institution of the century."[14] Citing his signed confidentiality agreement, the Pinkertons sued and seized the publisher's plates for the book. No one was allowed to write about being a Pinkerton except the Pinkerton family and their ghostwriters.

By 1915, when Sam Hammett answered the ad and joined its relatively recent Baltimore office, Pinkerton's had twenty branches in North America. The founder had always feared losing control of his company by expanding, with corruption a strong temptation in far-flung offices. Yet, following his death, the sons established outposts West of Chicago, in Denver and Spokane, and moved south into Baltimore and Washington,

D.C. By the time Hammett was hired, the demand for detective work had grown so that there were seventy-three different agencies in New York City alone. The rival Burns International Detective Agency had almost as many offices as Pinkerton's, and a headquarters in New York's gorgeous new Woolworth Building. And while the price to become an amateur detective through a popular correspondence school was $7.50, a beginning operative such as Hammett made only $21.00 per week. Still, "I liked gumshoeing," he said, "better than anything I had done before."[15]

Chapter II

A COMPANY MAN

It will not do to follow a person on the opposite side of the street, or close behind him, and when he stops to speak to a friend stop also; or if a person goes into a saloon, or store, pop in after him, stand staring till he goes out, and then follow him again. Of course such a "shadow" would be detected in fifteen minutes.

—ALLAN PINKERTON[1]

A WELL-TRAINED PINKERTON COULD keep shadowing in his sleep, when he was allowed any. Even while drugged with laudanum, Hammett's hard-traveled character the Continental Op trudges the dozens of American streets he's seen for the agency, names that Hammett likely unearthed from his own humble experience: Gay Street and Mount Royal Avenue in Baltimore, Colfax Avenue in Denver, McKinney Avenue in Dallas. Hammett seems to have been an adept shadow man from early on, as he was later happy to explain to his editor:

[A] detective may shadow a man for days and in the end have but the haziest idea of the man's features. Tricks of carriage, ways of wearing clothes, general outline, individual mannerisms—all as seen from the rear—are much more important to the shadow than faces. They can be recognized at a greater distance, and do not necessitate his getting in front of his subject at any time.[2]

For young shadow men starting out when Sam Hammett did, Pinkerton's had company pamphlets to explain the house style for every surveillance setting, from basic street shadowing to "railroad checking": "[operatives] should be provided with a suitable pretext such as salesman."[3] Separate pamphlets detailed the methods of stealing from streetcar boxes, how to examine steamer trunks on trains or monitor a railroad commissary for waste, theft, or doctored checks.[4] Every aspect of a Pinkerton's appearance was thought through, down to his luggage: "A brief case will often answer the purpose for daylight runs, but no operative should travel in a Pullman without a bag or suitcase."[5]

In Hammett's story "Who Killed Bob Teal?" a younger detective who is "well along the way to expertness" after only two years at the agency is killed by a bullet. Hammett survived his own apprenticeship, and one of the first men to help him along the way to expertness may have been his supervisor in the Baltimore office, an experienced Pinkerton whom Hammett later called James or Jimmy Wright and sometimes credited as the model for his fictional Continental Op. Many biographies and treatises have cited the importance of Wright to Hammett's development as a man and, ultimately, a writer. The trouble with this view is that no one has ever found proof of the elusive mentor Jimmy Wright. There seems little doubt that Hammett learned many of his skills and codes of detective conduct while employed with the Baltimore Pinkerton office, but Wright himself might be a bit of misdirection, a character as fictitious as Bob Teal.

In fact, "James Wright" had long been a popular alias with Pinkertons working undercover.[6] The code name appears as far back as 1874, when a St. Louis Pinkerton (John Boyle) traveling as "Mr. James Wright" rode with a former Chicago police captain (Louis J. Lull) going by W. J. Allen (echoing Allan Pinkerton's wartime alias). With a local lawman as guide, the two Pinkertons posed as land prospectors while trailing the Younger brothers in Missouri the same month that operative J. W. Whicher was murdered there by the James-Younger gang. The Youngers were staying in a rural farmhouse in St. Clair County, watching from the attic, when they noticed three well-armed strangers passing on the country road. Riding hard, the Youngers came up behind James Wright and his two colleagues. Wright galloped away as guns were drawn and had his hat blasted off by the Youngers as he rode out of view.* He left the other two men behind to face the brothers; one of them, Lull, produced a hidden Smith & Wesson and shot John Younger through the throat before being hit himself. Younger and Deputy Ed Daniels, the agent's guide, were killed in the melee, but Lull crawled away and lingered long enough to give a sworn account of the showdown before he died.

---

* Shorter accounts often give this honor to Jesse James, but the authoritative biography by T. J. Stiles, *Jesse James: Last Rebel of the Civil War*, (New York: Vintage, 2005), gives it to the Youngers, pp. 255–56.

"James Wright" lived to ride another day for Pinkerton's.

★   ★   ★

As a detective, Hammett was a company man like his Op, a foot soldier in an army of detecting. During Hammett's time, an operative might see a whole case through or merely snippets of it, as the Pinkerton agency rotated its scores of regional operatives in and out as needed. "Ninety-nine per cent of detective work is a patient collecting of details—and your details must be got as nearly first-hand as possible," says the Op in Hammett's story "One Hour."

Operative reports were meant to show clients how much daily investigating they were getting for their fee. As in news writing, the reports captured the "who, what, when, and where," with more expansive characterizations reserved for office memos such as this 1901 sketch of a post office thief: "'Figgsey' Lyons has made his home in Newark for some time and can be found any day in the Newark City Library, reading over the Cincinnati Inquirer for western news in regard to the doings of crooks."[7]

The Pinkerton archive at the Library of Congress lives in the Madison Building, near the Capitol, and holds sixty thousand documents and several hundred boxes of operative reports, along with agency employee records, memos on field agent salaries, cipher books, cables to clients, brochures for early listening devices (the Burns agency's "Detecti-Fone") or the patented Pinkerton "Photo Cabinet" (1917), a roll-top affair that law enforcement agencies could buy and fill with thousands of the latest mug shots.

As rich a trove as the archive is, no writing by Hammett has ever been identified within it; his reports either were submitted anonymously to client companies or have since been lost to fire or time. All materials from the offices where he worked longest, Baltimore and San Francisco, are also sadly missing, and very few unflattering records of strikebreaking cases were included when the collection was donated. (These purges could have been made in the 1930s, when the Agency was worried about being called before Congress for union busting under the new National Labor Relations Act.)

But even an hour spent reading through the reports of other operatives gives a good idea of the experiences and format that formed Hammett as a writer. For a general education in the details of a typical Pinkerton's life, there are many letters and directives out of the New York and Chicago offices (the latter in spite of the Great Chicago Fire) and memorable paperwork from ops working out of the Kansas City, Pittsburgh, or Spokane branches, enough to make plain what was expected in Hammett's day.*

Pinkertons were cautioned not to begin a case with a hasty theory, and their reports were written to a certain understated standard, presenting a collection of rogues rendered matter-of-factly, with a surprisingly light touch, though often their work was edited before being sent on to the client.

Pinkerton supervisors routinely functioned as editors, revising operatives' reports to please clients, somewhat the way a rewrite desk in a newspaper city room polished the eyewitness stories filed by "legmen." As Hammett explained, "A detective

---

* Documents were returned if the client was a private individual, an archivist who worked on the collection told me. The stated company policy was to return documents to the client once the case was closed.

official in San Francisco once substituted 'truthful' for 'voracious' in one of my reports on the grounds that the client might not understand the latter. A few days later in another report 'simulate' became 'quicken' for the same reason." It is not surprising that a writer who was later proud of his ability to sneak bits of gamey street parlance past his editors would have started out learning to improve his reports for Pinkerton clients. In *Red Harvest*, his Continental Op grouses about dressing up field reports for his old-school boss, "I might just as well have saved the labor and sweat I had put into trying to make my reports harmless. They didn't fool the Old Man. He gave me merry hell."

A single celebrated murder case from just before the Great War makes clear the breadth of investigation the Agency could bring to bear, and the kind of shadow work expected in Hammett's day. As an operative, Hammett did jobs just like these: watching a wealthy gentleman's Pullman berth overnight, tipping a porter to pluck a telegram from a subject's trash basket, chatting up gossipy landladies, or minding the driveway of a robbery suspect who was dumb enough to return home. Months and years were spent sharpening the habits of suspicious observation. Combined from multiple op reports, the investigation of the Rice murder makes an interesting detective story on its own.

William Lowe Rice was a successful corporate lawyer living in an elegant subdivision he'd helped pioneer, Cleveland Heights. He was an athletic man nearing fifty whose wife and daughters had gone ahead of him to the family's summer house on Cape Cod. On the evening of Friday, August 5, 1910, after playing nine holes at the Euclid Golf Club and dining and drinking there with friends until about ten thirty, he started to walk the five hundred yards along Overlook Road to his pillared brick colonial home, Lowe Ridge. On the road, Rice encountered several men beneath a street lamp who were described by others as having dark, curly hair and soft hats.

An altercation followed and the lawyer lay dying minutes later, when two automobiles stopped to investigate the still figure lying by the road. His jewelry and more than a hundred dollars cash were left on him; his body cut, bruised, and shot; a gold penknife lying open as if from a slashing fight. (His panama hat was also found nearby, with two bullet tears in it.) Two doctors out driving with their wives brought Rice to the hospital, where he died without a word. Rice's law partner then sent a telegram to a Pinkerton supervisor: PLEASE SEND FIRST TRAIN YOUR VERY BEST AND MOST EXPERIENCED MAN TO PUT IN RICE CASE. NO ORDINARY MAN, BUT ONE ACCUSTOMED TO SUCH CASES.

Operatives interviewed streetcar workers who might have seen the bloodied killer in the hours after William Rice died. "I can see it in my mind's eye just like a picture," a brakeman recalled. "He was sitting on the south side of the car in the smoker just behind me, leaning his head on his hand.'"[8] On learning that dark, "foreign"-looking men had been seen on the road just before Rice was killed, Pinkerton's sent in its own Sicilian agents to secure rooms in Italian boardinghouses.

On August 7, a day and a half after the crime, operative C. Y. Riddle arrived in Cleveland Heights with a flourish: "I alighted from a Euclid car at Lake View and walked up through Mayfield Road, known as Little Italy, to Overlook Road and over the scene of the murder." An experienced op like those

Hammett would later sketch, Riddle cast a cold eye over clues that proved irrelevant, even a bloodstained handkerchief:

> The handkerchief is of a cheap variety with blue and white border, but the stains look old as though rain had fallen since it had laid there. I also found a piece of a collar band from a black stripped shirt. It had been partly torn and cut away from the shirt and had the letters "Ben" on the band but this was too old to have belonged to anyone connected with this crime.[9]

After kicking through some bushes, Riddle learned about a burlap bag full of seven dead chickens found 150 feet west of where Rice had died. Examining the bag, he noticed a copper band on a hen's leg from the coop of one of Rice's neighbors.

The discovery of the dead chickens led the Pinkertons to theorize that the killers were a group of Italian laborers who had been out grabbing hens for the upcoming Festival of San Giuseppe when they were discovered by Rice, which led to a fatal struggle. Operatives took the burlap bag around to Italian dry goods stores to trace its ownership. But to some people, given Rice's wealth and impressive collection of enemies, the chicken-thief theory seemed too random and squalid a death, especially to Rice's family. When it came out at the inquest that another of his neighbors, John Hartness Brown, had appeared at the crime scene moments after the killing and unceremoniously helped get Rice's body into the doctor's car, he became a more fitting suspect.

Brown's rivalry and business grievances with Rice were gossiped about, and so, two weeks after the crime, on the night of Saturday, August 20, 1910, Pinkerton operative J. V. O'Neill

shadowed Brown, a thickset, red-faced man about forty-five
years old and six feet tall, on an overnight train from Cleveland
to Boston:

> During the night I kept close watch on Mr. Brown's berth in
> anticipation of his leaving the train. However, I did not see
> him until after the train had left Albany, N.Y. He then arose,
> made his toilet, and had his breakfast in the dining car . . . I
> interviewed the conductor with a view of learning for a
> certainty Mr. Brown's destination."[10]

At Springfield, Brown sent a telegram advising someone
when he'd arrive in Boston. Operative O'Neill learned from
the porter that Brown had begun a separate telegram announ-
cing he'd be at the Hotel Touraine, and then substituted
the other message. When the train stopped at Worcester,
Massachusetts, two other Pinkertons boarded the car, instruc-
ted to look for a florid-faced man wearing spectacles and a split
straw hat. O'Neill pointed out their subject, and operative
C. B. Patterson started his watch:

> The train arrived in Boston at 11.50 A.M. and Brown, carry-
> ing a black suit case, a black bag and a tan leather extension
> bag like a steamer trunk, boarded a taxicab at the South
> Station, rode to Hotel Touraine, and registered at 12.05 P.M.[11]

After ordering some liquor to be sent to Rockland, Maine,
Brown returned to his hotel with another man in a straw hat
and gray suit, then began a complex series of maneuvers, as if
aware of his shadow, before leaving Boston on the night train

to Rockland. The investigation moved back to the chicken thieves.

A murder weapon eventually was found in the Rice case—the softness of the recovered bullet had suggested a foreign make—and over the coming months, through constant shadowing of the suspects' wives, two Cleveland men, Vincenzo Pelato and Pietro Tomasello, were traced to Brooklyn, New York, and Black Diamond, California.

Pelato broke first, placing the blame for the shooting on Tomasello, who was interrogated for eight hours in February 1912 in the Columbus, Ohio, penitentiary. Having countered the suspect's every denial, at 5:00 P.M. Francis Dimaio, the arresting Pinkerton superintendent who spent two years working the Rice case, produced the big foreign pistol that had shot William Rice. "When was the last time you saw this?" Dimaio asked Tomasello, who collapsed into "hysterics," according to witnesses, until the prison doctor had to calm him with a "sleeping potion."

The men were convicted of robbery before murder charges could be brought. Whether Rice's neighbor William Hartness Brown had hired the killers or Rice just died confronting a gang of chicken thieves was never proven in court.* (Brown survived public suspicion and moved to England.) But Dimaio cleared it up late in his life, nearing ninety when he wrote to his old agency colleagues about the real shooter:

---

* When the Cleveland *Plain Dealer* revisited the infamous case in 1941, the writer offered the theory that Rice had been killed because he was changing his will, as well as a possibility that he'd been mistaken for neighbor Brown, the alleged true target of the Italian assassins.

[County Detective]Doran and I traced the [chicken] bag . . .
to a feed store in East Cleveland who told us that the bag in
question had been sent to the Sciarabba brothers . . . When
we went to find them, I secured from an Italian informant, a
neighbor of the Sciarabba brothers, that they were the actual
murderers of Attorney Rice, but had left town and were
then in Brazil."[12]

One of the Sciarabbas had fired as Rice wrestled and traded
knife slashes with his first attacker. But having no extradition
treaty with Brazil, they prosecuted the two witnesses to the
murder (Pelato and Tomasello), who were eventually released
despite their confession.

Beyond the collective failure of all those hardworking
Pinkertons, it is interesting how familiar such reports sound
from the Hammett style they later inspired: hopping streetcars,
watching houses, quizzing neighbors, blind turns taken that
nevertheless seem to add momentum, investigative failures
that lend realism. Before he could write his fictional Op stories,
Hammett read and submitted scores of such memos on the job.
"Thanks to my ability to write pleasing and convincing
reports," he said, "my reputation was always a little more than
I deserved."[13]

Chapter III

$5,000 BLOOD MONEY

*I dug out my card case and ran through the collection
of credentials I had picked up here and there by one
means or another. The red card was the one I wanted.
It identified me as Henry F. Neill, A.B. seaman,
member in good standing of the Industrial Workers of
the World. There wasn't a word of truth in it.*

— *RED HARVEST* (1929)

IT'S NEARLY FOUR MILES from the train depot, where
Frank Little arrived in Butte, Montana in July 1917, up Main
Street to the hilltop cemetery where he was buried less than
three weeks later. Much of it is steep going, along an incline
that builds to a heady view of the copper pits and disused head-
frames and the magnificence of the surrounding Rockies. It
was dusty and hot in the summer of 1917, with a low haze
hanging over the town and an escalating tension between
Butte's striking mine workers and the Anaconda Copper
Mining Company. This tinderish state of affairs had caught
Frank Little's imagination.

Little entered town on crutches. A professional bringer of chaos, he wore his Stetson angled and proudly called himself a "half-breed." At five foot ten, he had dark hair, one working eye, and a blunt face whose mouth curled up on one side in a defiant smirk. At thirty-eight, he was a well-worn and unlikable veteran of many campaigns for the International Workers of the World, for whom he'd been stomped, kidnapped, often jailed, and very nearly hanged. He'd recently broken his ankle in a car accident while agitating in Minnesota, then spent the last few weeks on a strike in Bisbee, Arizona, which ended with hundreds of workers being deported by cattle car into the New Mexican desert. He often boasted of his willingness to face a firing squad, and for inspiration, he carried a small pouch of ashes of the recently martyred Wobbly organizer Joe Hill.

Volatility long preceded Little's arrival in Butte. A union hall had been dynamited and federal troops summoned there during labor violence three years before, and in early June 1917, the town saw draft riots, followed days later by the largest hard-rock mining disaster in American history. An underground fire began on June 8 in the Granite Mountain shaft and eventually left 163 men dead. Fifteen thousand surviving miners went out on strike as scores of Pinkerton and Brown detectives roamed the town, spying and intimidating on behalf of the mining company, along with other well-armed guards.[1] One Pinkerton who later recalled wandering Butte that summer was a young operative from the Baltimore office named Sam Hammett. He often told the story of being there in 1917 and how he was offered five thousand dollars to kill the Wobbly agitator Frank Little.

When Little reached Butte during the latest strike in mid-July, the new miners' union was still unrecognized and unaffiliated. He hoped to make turmoil out of the standoff and deliver the strikers to the IWW. Though hobbled and half-blind, Little was considered a dangerous man when he checked into a boardinghouse near Finlander Hall, where he was to speak next day. He did not disappoint, denouncing the American war effort as a capitalist slaughterfest and calling doughboys on their way to Europe "Uncle Sam's scabs in uniform." His comments were seized on by reporters for Butte's company-owned newspapers, whom he came to address as the "prostitutes of the press." Over the coming days he continued to inspire and inflame, stumping for worldwide revolution and bringing calls for him to be muzzled under the new wartime Espionage Act. Montana's federal district attorney, Burton K. Wheeler, an independent-minded son of eastern Quaker parents, determined that Little's rantings against the war may have been distasteful but he could not legally stop him. In the early hours of August 1, a black Cadillac carrying six masked men came for Little instead.

They parked before number 316 North Wyoming Street, an address that is today the low-slung Capri Inn, on the western edge of the city. One of the men watched the street, while the other five entered the building and stove in the door of room number 30, which was empty. This woke the landlady, sleeping in the room next door, to whom one of the strangers explained, "We are officers and we are after Frank Little."[2] When she told them they had the wrong room, they broke in the door to number 32, where they found the agitator asleep in his leg cast and underwear. Before Little could reach his crutches propped against the bed they had seized him, gagged his mouth with a towel, and hauled him from the house. The landlady called the police station to explain that masked officers had just carried off the man they meant to "deport." The policeman on the phone did not know of any department business with Little and dispatched three men to check on the matter.

By this time, Little had been tied to the rear bumper of his abductors' car and dragged behind it for a block, scraping off much of his kneecaps (as photos would ghoulishly show). The men then pulled him up to be hanged from the Milwaukee railroad trestle on the southern outskirts, near the Centennial Brewery. Either before or after Little died, the killers pinned a message written in red lettering to his underwear:

OTHERS TAKE

NOTICE!

FIRST AND LAST

WARNING!

3-7-77

Ⓛ- D- C- S- S- W- T

The numbers 3-7-77, possibly designating the standard dimensions for a grave, were a well-known vigilante symbol of Montana frontier justice, a coffin notice painted on a man's door as a warning to leave town. (They appear on official Montana State Trooper patches to this day.[3]) The letters at the bottom of the message were broadly interpreted as standing for the names of strike leaders marked for removal, with the *L* for "Little" definitively circled.

On August 5, three thousand people walked Frank Little's casket up to Mountain Meadow Cemetery. Ten days after the murder, federal troops again entered Butte (as they had in 1914). The strike collapsed that fall, and troops remained until the end of the war, guarding the production of copper. The killers, popularly suspected as hired by the Anaconda Mining Company, were never found.

The story of Frank Little and the deadly bribe became a favorite of Hammett's, usually drawing the aghast reaction he was after. Lillian Hellman first heard it not long after meeting Hammett in Hollywood in 1930 and recorded the story years later in her memoir *Scoundrel Time*:

> I remember sitting on a bed next to him in the first months we met, listening to him tell me about his Pinkerton days when an officer of Anaconda Copper Company had offered him five thousand dollars to kill Frank Little, the labor union organizer. I didn't know Hammett well enough to hear the anger under the calm voice, the bitterness under the laughter, so I said, "He couldn't have made such an offer unless you had been strike-breaking for Pinkerton."
>
> "That's about right," he said.

The idea that he had been a strikebreaker seemed to offend Hellman at least as much as the deadly import of the bribe, but "through the years," she wrote, "he was to repeat that bribe offer so many times that I came to believe, knowing him now, that it was a kind of key to his life. He had given a man the right to think he would murder."[4] Not only was the story true, she decided, it had stamped him permanently. "I think I can date Hammett's belief that he was living in a corrupt society from Little's murder."[5]

Although he had seen plenty of corruption, chances are Hammett never laid eyes on Frank Little, living or dead, beyond the autopsy picture and death mask that ran in newspapers that fatal week.* On the face of it, a relatively recent hire out of the Baltimore office would seem an unlikely choice for the assassination of a Wobbly leader; Pinkerton's secret operatives in Butte were assigned primarily out of its Denver and Spokane offices; and the money (five thousand dollars) seems suspiciously high, even if Hammett was offered the job solo. Little had already survived one attempted lynching, and Anaconda had its pick of dozens of more qualified hired thugs to kill him that summer. The only person who offered the job to Hammett seems to have been Hammett himself, in a bar tale that showed the hallmarks of his writing craft—inserting himself just far enough to be plausible, not claiming he'd been a full party to the killing but elegantly cloaking his story in its atmosphere.

But Hammett didn't need to see that particular conflict that summer to experience brutality and corruption as a Pinkerton. He'd already served as a paid combatant in other labor skirmishes, learning from these that even when a client was despicable, the detective's first loyalty was to the job. Retelling the Little incident doubtless evoked some ugly strikebreaking stints of his own.

While assembling material for her memoir, *Dashiell Hammett: A Daughter Remembers* (2001), Jo Hammett received several boxes of old family photos, including an uncaptioned group portrait of her father among a tough work crew standing by a railroad siding, one of the men wearing a wide-brimmed hat and brandishing a switch.[6] Her guess is that it is probably a

---

* These are today on file at the beautiful Butte–Silver Bow Public Archives, a bright converted fire station building on West Quartz Street, along the uphill route of Little's funeral procession.

group of Pinkerton strikebreakers, possibly taken in the late teens, hired to go to work on someone with these long, cut switches, or "saps," a small glimpse of the rough tasks the agency dispatched Hammett to perform in these early years.

There is no evidence beyond his own word that he was in Butte in 1917, but it is possible he visited in 1920, when he worked for several months out of the Spokane office and Pinkerton's was employed in yet another battle between the miners and the Anaconda Company.* Later living in one of America's most beautiful cities, he would place his first novel in a grimy violent boomtown very much like Butte, "an ugly city . . . set in an ugly notch between two ugly mountains that had been all dirtied up by mining."[7] In *Red Harvest* the detective burns down much of the town to free it, using hell-raising techniques cribbed from agitators like Frank Little.

★ ★ ★

DURING HIS FIRST two years as a Pinkerton, Hammett traveled extensively around the South and Midwest, but was still living with his parents and brother and sister in Baltimore when, on April 2, 1917, Woodrow Wilson asked Congress to declare war on Germany. As a young, unattached man over twenty-one years old, Sam Hammett qualified for the first round of national

---

* The strongest argument I've come across is the one advanced in a 1982 paper by the Moscow, Idaho, bookstore owner Robert Greene: A detective named Hammett takes part in the death of a suspect in Upton Sinclair's 1920 protest novel, *100%: The Story of a Patriot*. But even if the two men had met in the teens and Sinclair heard it from Hammett's own lips, it would not prove that he took part in the crime or that he was even in Butte that summer. Still, Greene's view of Hammett as a writer seeking absolution for his crimes is an interesting one also taken up by the crime writer James Ellroy.

draft registrations on June 5. The registrar inspecting him in Baltimore may have looked skeptically at the young man's willowy build (noting his "slender" frame on his draft card), but was reassured by his hardy-sounding work experience as a Maryland "private detective" for Pinkerton's.* Given his quarrelsome relationship with his father, it is surprising that Hammett had not long since left home, unless a combination of economic necessity and basic loafishness kept him home. But on June 24, 1918, fourteen months after America had joined the war, he took his leave from Pinkerton's and entered the army.

He was twenty-four years old when he reported as a private to Camp Meade, a newly established cantonment outside Baltimore. He was less than twenty miles from his family but leaving home at last. Although there were just five months before the Armistice, Hammett would be as dramatically affected by his months in the military as would Ernest Hemingway, who that spring had suspended his own apprenticeship as a reporter for the *Kansas City Star* to join the Red Cross ambulance volunteers in Italy. Each man would spend much of his war in a hospital bed. "I contributed practically nothing to the Allied victory," Hammett assured a reporter. "I came out of my uniform with tuberculosis."

---

* Hammett's draft registration card is from June 5, 1917, when he was unattached and well of age at twenty-three, and was not a member of an essential occupation excused from the first round of registration. Unlike the later draft that used the mails, most men registered for the system in person, on designated registration days, and then entered the services after their number was later posted. Hammett's draft card is one of two legal documents where he names Pinkerton's as his employer.

Chapter IV

OUT OF UNIFORM

C AMP MEADE WAS only months old, one of sixteen Army cantonments thrown up in a patriotic frenzy of digging, sawing, and hammering in the weeks after Wilson's appeal to Congress that spring. It still smelled of fresh wood when the first new draftees began reporting even before many outbuildings were finished, and by October 1917, some twenty-three thousand men filled the camp, where more than a hundred thousand soldiers would be trained by war's end.

Hammett arrived at Camp Meade as a private. On July 12, following basic training, he was assigned to Motor Ambulance Corps Number Forty-Nine and began helping to shuttle sick and wounded soldiers, many returned from Europe, to the hospital. Out of this job would come two formative tragedies.

The big boxy Fords and GMs outfitted for the army's new ambulance corps were an improvement over the horse-drawn wagons they were replacing, but they were also clumsy for driving, even in camp, far from the European front; their high wheels were good for crossing streams in a hurry but left the vehicles tippy when stacked full with patients. Volunteers operating the motor ambulances close to the European fighting employed some tricky maneuvering; to get around the challenges of the Ford's gravity-fed gasoline system, which made it prone to stall on steep grades, some drove uphill in reverse. The brakes were also not designed for mountains, according to an army historian: "Drivers kept an eye peeled for strategically placed trees that could stop them if necessary. Sometimes patients had unforgettable rides."[1]

Sometime that summer or early fall, Hammett would remember, he was driving an ambulance filled with wounded soldiers when it flipped over, with a terrible result: the men were thrown out onto the roadside. "He hit a rock or something and dumped the patients and he never touched a car after that," remembered his daughter Mary, born well after the war. "He refused to drive, absolutely refused to drive." As hazardous as these ambulance coaches were to maneuver, however, nine decades later no record can be found of Hammett's traumatic accident at Meade. But the fact remains that, after the war, he almost never got behind the wheel if he could avoid it, citing this painful memory. Whatever the reason, something spooked him about driving, and in later years the wartime incident may also have served as a more manly sounding explanation when his illness left him too weak to safely operate a car.

Of the second episode at Meade there can be no doubt, since it was part of a much wider calamity that came on the heels of the world war: a deadly influenza in 1918–19 that killed many times more human beings than the Great War itself, claiming between twenty and forty million victims worldwide. It infected more than a quarter of all Americans, of whom some 675,000 died—a virus unprecedented for its deadly range, striking down people in their prime more than just the very young and old. A feverish young boy could go to sleep comforted by his mother, only to wake hours later to find she had been taken by the flu instead. It was a nightmarish, wracking death, from which victims often died after turning dark blue from choking on what a doctor called "a blood-tinged froth."

The war and its network of army camps, featuring large clusters of men and their frequent deployments, sped the contagion along. "One in every sixty-seven soldiers in the army died of influenza and its complications," the historian John M. Barry has pointed out, "nearly all of them in a ten-week period beginning in mid-September."[2] First appearing in the Midwest that spring, the virus infected men at Camp Funston in Kansas before traveling to the port city of Brest, France, loosed in a country where two million American servicemen were stationed. A more virulent strain returned to the States that fall. In early September, sick sailors aboard the *Harold Walker* left Boston for the Philadelphia Navy Yard, with others sailing on to deliver the virus to New Orleans and Mexico. By October 4, almost five thousand men were sick at Illinois's Camp Grant, with four hundred and five hundred deaths daily; while at Camp Devens, outside Boston, fifteen hundred soldiers were reported ill on a single day. After seeing dozens of soldiers die, an army physician laid out the flu's awful stages for a colleague:

> Two hours after admission they have the mahogany spots over the cheek bones, and a few hours later you can begin to see the Cyanosis extending from their ears and spreading all over the face until it is difficult to distinguish the colored men from the white.[3]

In mid-September, the influenza had turned up at Camps Dix and Meade, the two cantonments nearest the wildly infected city of Philadelphia. Working in the ambulances, Hammett of course would have been regularly exposed to the virus as he delivered feverish soldiers to the infirmary. On October 6, three weeks after the virus reached camp, he fell ill himself, reporting a high temperature and chronic cough. (His medical report lists pneumonia, situated in his lower right lung.) He was shortly transferred from a field to a base hospital, where he spent eight days unable even to sit up in bed. After twenty days, he was returned to active service, weak and emaciated, his rib cage wracked and lungs frayed; but unlike the scores of soldiers carried from infirmaries to morgues, he was unmistakably alive. He had survived what was then his closest brush with death, yet had little idea the full extent to which it had broken down his body.[4]

"I have always had good health until I contracted influenza," he would tell an army clinician. By February 1919, he was back in the camp hospital with "acute bronchitis," complaining of a lasting cough and morning soreness in his throat. The symptoms were treated straightforwardly as lingering inflammation, an aftereffect, and Hammett returned to duty after four days in the hospital. By late April, he had made sergeant. In the group photo taken that month with the men of his ambulance corps he looks almost healthful, his face not especially gaunt beneath the rim of his doughboy hat. But he was back in the hospital on May 29, his breathing labored and leaving him dizzy. He had night sweats.[5]

This time doctors pronounced his condition untreatable: he had tuberculosis, they said, caught during his army service. He was judged 25 percent disabled, and a medical discharge was recommended that same day.

In fact, though he likely contracted it in the army, Hammett had possibly been exposed to the disease first as a child. His mother's cough was a familiar sound around the house, leading some to speculate that his wartime bout of influenza had possibly weakened him enough to waken a long dormant strain of TB. "Primary" TB, however, as opposed to "reactivation" TB, starts in the lower lobes of the lungs, as Hammett's seemed to, attacking his already weakened respiratory system.[6] Certainly the army believed he had contracted it in camp. On May 30, 1919, he left the army as a sergeant with an honorable discharge and a small pension, a twenty-five-year-old former shadow man now too short-winded to climb a set of stairs. Hammett came home a disabled veteran of a war he had never seen, whose fighting he had heard about from wounded men in his ambulance. He was back with his parents after less than a year, his health wrecked, but hoping somehow to return to work as a detective.

At the time of his diagnosis, tuberculosis was no longer the romantic-sounding "consumption" that had taken John Keats, the affliction that sent patients for enforced rest in the country, where they often died out of sight. Ever since 1882, when Robert Koch spotted "beautifully blue" *tubercle bacilli* among the brown animal tissue under his microscope, it had been known as an often deadly communicable disease of the poor, transmitted among passengers in steerage, tenants packed in overcrowded slums, or, in Hammett's case, from cot to cot in a teeming army hospital. It was no less deadly a disease than before Koch's discovery, but now carried a more shameful stigma because of its communicability. It was the mark of the patient's marginality, and even if a person's health seemed to return, there was always the specter of a hacking end in which the body withered and the lungs filled with blood.

It was no wonder that Hammett chose to make the most of his time between relapses. "His illness caused him to conclude that it was useless to take good care of yourself," wrote his daughter Jo. "He told me that the guys in the army hospital who followed the doctor's orders, got lots of rest and good nights' sleep, did worse than those like himself who sneaked out to town and smoked, drank, and helled around when they could. He believed that the disease respected toughness, a quality that my father admired greatly."[7] Hammett made very few decisions in favor of his health, smoking and drinking when he was strong enough, feeling, as many "lungers" understandably did, that his present life was borrowed and his future short and deadly.

During his time away, Hammett's parents had moved nearby to a house on West Lexington Street. Although he appears in the city directory at this address only as "salesman," he probably did part-time work for Pinkerton's, as his strength permitted, to supplement his pension. In December 1919 his health again worsened, army doctors pronounced him 50 percent disabled, and his pension was raised to forty dollars per month. Over the first few months of the New Year came another ebbing of his symptoms, and by May his tuberculosis had receded enough that he seized the chance to set out on his own.

He headed all the way to Spokane, Washington, a fast-growing northern rail center whose population had just passed one hundred thousand, earning it a new outpost of Pinkerton's

National Detective Agency—a promise of work if Hammett's body held out. The wet cold of the Pacific Northwest wasn't necessarily better for Hammett's lungs, but over the few months before his health crashed again he collected a number of detecting adventures he would later exploit—in the mining country, on the ranches, in small towns in Washington, in Oregon, or in Montana, where he transported a prisoner outside a dying gold mining town:

> Taking a prisoner from a ranch near Gilt Edge, Mont., to Lewiston one night, my machine broke down and we had to sit there until daylight. The prisoner, who stoutly affirmed his innocence, was clothed only in overalls and shirt. After shivering all night on the front seat his morale was low, and I had no difficulty in getting a complete confession from him while walking to the nearest ranch early the following morning.[8]

From early on, Hammett knew how to make his sketches more believable with a mix of street knowledge and self-deprecation, an approach that gained him the benefit of the reader's doubt, whether the story was about his achieving a confession from a chilled prisoner in a broken-down car or going undercover as a member of the Civic Purity League.

After his months in Spokane and Seattle, the operative's life again proved too much, and by October 1920, when his weight had dropped from around 150 pounds to 132, he was complaining once more of weakness and a shortness of breath. He was again hospitalized for "pulminary tuberculosis."[9] Until then, each breakdown in his health had taken something away—his livelihood as a full-time Pinkerton, his army career—but with his transfer to a new sanitarium outside Tacoma, his awful disease would finally add something wonderful to his existence.

Chapter V

DEAREST WOMAN

Some day I may partially forget you, and be able to enjoy another woman, but there's nothing to show that it'll be soon. If anything, I'm a damnder fool now than I ever was.

—SAM HAMMETT TO JOSEPHINE ANNIS DOLAN, 1921

THERE WAS NOTHING uncommon about a patient taking an interest in one of the young women in white pinafores cheerfully coming in and out of his room. Their visits were the high point of any recovering serviceman's routine, and the women were all too used to the male attention; a certain amount of flirty banter even helped move the day along. Thousands of men had fallen for their nurses during the war, and while the more experienced ones had learned to deflect the romantic chatter, occasionally a soldier's persistence kindled more than sympathy. Even without the disease that altered his life, Hammett still might have later tried his hand at writing, but he certainly would never have met Josephine Annis Dolan, an army nurse with a second lieutenant's rank, who caught the eye of every young man whose life she enriched on her rounds.

The place where the two came together was a converted Indian trade school on the outskirts of Tacoma that had chiefly served the Puyallup tribe. Before its conversion, the fifty-year-old Cushman Indian Trades School had already been on the decline when it was hit hard by the influenza epidemic in 1919, went bankrupt, and was closed. By the fall of 1920, Hammett was among the healthier of the two hundred patients at the repurposed facility, the Cushman Institute: "[T]he Veterans Administration hadn't any hospitals of its own in those days," he wrote in *Tulip*, "so the United States Public Health Service took care of us in its hospitals. In this one about half of us were lungers, the other half what was then called shell shock victims, segregated as far as sleeping quarters and eating were concerned."

Tall, clean, charming, and neatly dressed, Hammett even made his own bed, all of which was noticed by his admiring young nurse. Of all the guests there, "he seemed to stand out," she recalled. "He always dressed so beautifully, and the area where he slept was very neat. He wasn't very sick then, and he helped the other patients." Josephine, called Jose,* was soon so taken with the handsome newcomer that she chose not to believe Hammett had tuberculosis, which she knew could be fatal as well as contagious, but had merely been sent to recover from the influenza. Soon the two were sneaking out together, onto the bridge, to the parks, out for a ferry ride or a long dinner in Tacoma at the Peerless Grill. She was a nurse like his

---

* Like "Joe's."

mother, but unlike Annie Hammett, who was largely house-bound, she had been on her own since she was fifteen. Soon the Pinkerton shadow man was following after his nurse on her rounds, making himself useful.

In later years, Hammett attempted to write about an appealing young nurse and her patient, but he could not set down his full feelings as he did in his early letters to Jose.[1] These reflect a young man in love, perhaps for the first time, unburdening himself in a way later made impossible by the hard-boiled style he would perfect. He came to write to her as the man he hoped to be—calling her Dear Nurse, Little Chap, Dear Lady, Little Fellow, Josephine Anna, "dearest small person in the world," Dear Boss, Little Handful, and Dearest Woman, and signing off as Sam, S.D.H., Daddy L.L., or Hammett.

When Hammett first saw her, Josephine was three years his junior, twenty-three, pretty, petite, and good at her job. She had been born in Basin, Montana and had the kind of childhood in which perhaps the nicest thing that had happened was her leaving the orphanage as a young girl. Unlike her handsome patient, she had clearly been in Butte and Anaconda during the labor violence of 1917, the great mine explosion, and the lynching of Frank Little, and as a second lieutenant in the army nursing corps, she outranked him. She had also been on her own longer, spending much of her life taking care of anyone who seemed small and vulnerable.

Jose's own parents had come to the rough mining country of the American West from other hardscrabble places: her father from the West Virginia coal country and her mother traveling from Ireland as a girl of sixteen. The couple had three children before Jose's mother, Maggie, died when Jose was three and a half. By the time Hubert Dolan, a hard-drinking miner, also passed on three years later, his youngest, a baby boy, had died before him. Josephine and her younger brother Walter entered a Catholic orphanage in Helena.

There she stayed for a year, protecting her little brother as best she could among the institution's harsh nuns, before her father's married sister in Anaconda, Alice Kelly, suffered a crisis of conscience in the form of a guilty dream. Josephine's dead mother, Maggie, appeared to Alice and pleaded with her to free her daughter from the orphanage, which she did, despite already having a very crowded houseful of her own children. (Walter was not rescued along with Jose, though he did survive.)

Jose was about seven when she came to live with her cousins the Kellys in Anaconda. "Captain" William Kelly was an executive in the Anaconda Copper Mining Company, and his house made an interesting vantage point for the local labor wars. She attended school through the eighth grade (just one grade less than Hammett) and entered nursing training at a Catholic hospital in Butte, where she endured a second round with strict nuns at fifteen. When America entered the war, she enlisted with a friend and saw some of the world beyond Montana, landing finally at the new sanitarium near Tacoma.

Remembering his months at Cushman years later, Hammett stressed the rowdy pastimes of the men, their late-night card games and dark pranks such as tossing metal trays clanging over the barrier to frighten the shell-shocked patients. Jose recalled instead the well-mannered man who liked to read when he wasn't following her around the grounds. In February 1921, after almost four months together, Hammett was transferred to another U.S. Public Health Service hospital, a stricter one at

Camp Kearney, outside San Diego, whose climate was thought
better for respiratory cases. "Which lunger are you taking out
now and dragging into town when he should be sleeping?" he
wrote his favorite nurse on February 27. "Or are you storing up
a little sleep before you start off again?"

On paper, it is a one-sided courtship. Hammett purged or
eventually lost Jose's letters to him, the very ones he clearly
suffered waiting for, but her coy, romantic confidence is implied
in his answers: "What I would like to write would be a letter of
the most passionate sort—one that would knock you off your
chair—but I remember you saying that you were going to cut
one bird off your list because his (your traveling man) letters
were too loving; so I think [I]'ll play safe."

Remembering Cushman, he wrote her in early March while
awaiting her next letter:

The worst part of the day is when the clock shows 740 P.M.,
and I know that I should be down in front of the office, in
the rain, waiting for Josephine Anna. Six O'Clock worries
me, also—occasionally, when I figure it's time for your
afternoon off and I should be standing on the People's Store
corner, still in the rain, cursing you because you are fifteen
minutes late and haven't shown up yet. I'll never awake at
eleven, or I reckon I'd be thinking we ought to be out on
the bridge—in the rain, of course—staging our customary
friendly, but now and then a bit rough, dispute over the
relative merits of "Yes" and "no."[2]

This dispute clearly went back and forth, at least sometimes
leaning toward yes. After hinting in several letters that she did

not feel well, Jose left Cushman for an unexplained visit home to her family in Anaconda. Following his hospital discharge, on June 2, 1921, Hammett wrote her from Spokane to explain his own plans. He was healthier but nearly broke, and the "fat heads" in charge of Camp Kearney had offered "a ticket to Spokane or nothing." He inquired innocently about the timetable for Jose's "vacation," and sometime later in June learned the truth behind her leaving her job. She was pregnant. The letter in which he discovered he would be a father is missing; nor does Jose seem to have saved his answer, in which he presumably offered to marry her. Perhaps she wasn't proud of the circumstances around her marriage, or simply didn't want to help her children figure out the math behind the proposal's timing. "I haven't any plans for the future," he wrote her that June, "but I reckon things will work out in some manner."[3]

From Spokane he went to Seattle for about a week, and then, if the Hammett-like narrator of his novel fragment *Tulip* is to be believed, he planned to visit San Francisco for perhaps two months "before going home to Baltimore." But he would never move back, staying on in San Francisco, a wide-open port town whose hills ran spectacularly down to the sea and whose people were taking the recent Volstead Act in easy stride in its wine flats and speakeasies. The town was run, in the grateful words of the city's most successful madame, by "municipal swashbucklers." This was probably the most beautiful place Hammett had ever been, a "sunpainted" town when the mists burned away, where he could find weekly fights at the Mission Armory, and trolleys and cable cars made it easier to do without an automobile.

"You're from San Francisco?" a character asks in one of his Op stories. "I remember the funny little streetcars, and the fog, and the salad right after the soup, and Coffee Dan's," a down-stairs speakeasy that guests entered by a slide and could beat the tables with wooden mallets if they liked the show. There was nothing like that in Spokane, Tacoma, Seattle, or Butte.

Hammett was thoroughly charmed by San Francisco, despite its being a steep city on foot, prone to a fog that was "thin, clammy, and penetrant," and not ideal for his recovery. But beyond its hillsides and mournful ferry horns it was home to a criminal class that was growing with Prohibition—rumrunners, racketeers, and high-living politicians—a range of characters irresistible to a man trained in the cultivation of crooks. The city's profitably lenient mayor, "Sunny Jim" Rolph, was a far cry from the dour preachers Hammett encountered elsewhere around the country. The combination made the town heady and attractive, if he could find any money for a family and his lungs improved. With nothing saved and having been in the hospital again since his discharge from Camp Kearney, Hammett asked Jose to join him in San Francisco and start their life together.

She came out by train from Montana the first week of July, and for chaste appearances he put up his pregnant fiancée in a hotel off Union Square, the Golden West (now Hotel Union Square), while they waited to get married. Hammett himself stayed in rooms across Ellis Street from Jose's hotel. The wedding ceremony occurred on July 7 at St. Mary's Cathedral,* in the rectory rather than the nave because Hammett was not

---

* Some errors about Josephine's family history were clearly introduced by Hammett himself while hurriedly filling out the marriage certificate, making the same mistake ("Josephine Anna" instead of "Annis") he had made in his love letters and mixing up her father's and mother's origins.

only undevout ("I haven't any God except Josephine," he'd written her) but also vague about whether he had been baptized (in fact, he had). Then the couple moved into a ten-year-old apartment building in the Tenderloin district, at 620 Eddy Street, the Crawford Apartments.

"I . . . brought my still-frayed lungs to San Francisco," he remembered, "and returned to sleuthing." In the Crawford Apartments, the couple would start their family life and Hammett, frayed lungs or not, would have a few more detecting adventures before he was invalided out.

Chapter VI

THE LAST CASE

*"Jerry Young," she repeated, as if to herself. "That's
a nice name. And you are the bootlegger?"*

"Not the," *I corrected. "Just* a. *This is San
Francisco."*

—"The Whosis Kid"

U P ON THE ROOF, where the couple liked to take pictures
with a box camera and where Jose would later bring
their young children to play in the sun, they could look out
across the rooftops at the beautiful city, so much of it built
new since the desolation of the great quake and fire in 1906.
Out there Hammett would set many of his bank heists, blackmail killings, and wandering-daughter cases in a wide swath
that curled around the couple's new home on Eddy Street, a
furnished three-room affair arranged along a skinny hallway.
Their landlady bootlegged on the side, as many now did, and
downstairs they heard patrons come and go in the night.

Four blocks away was the San Francisco public library, a
handy walk when Hammett's health behaved, an institution

filled with the raw materials for his continuing education in German criminology or medieval history, animal husbandry or the novels of Henry James, as well as its racks of pulp adventure magazines, whose daring sleuths often drew his professional contempt. The main reading room, with its high windows and long wooden tables, was a place of sanctuary away from the detectives' room or the happy noise of his family apartment.

For all its attractions, it is hard to imagine him getting around this hillside city he somehow learned to draw so surely, despite his bad lungs, climbing Telegraph Hill or walking over to the Latin Quarter or the ferry terminal and Embarcadero; riding the California cable line down into Chinatown, searching its alleys and "dark corners" behind the chop suey houses.

Eight long blocks from home was the James Flood Building, where he went to work again for Pinkerton's part time in the fall of 1921. A slight improvement in his health had gotten his disability pension halved to forty dollars per month, five dollars short of the couple's rent, and with a child due in October he returned to the familiar work of an operative, while petitioning the Veteran's Bureau to send him to secretarial school to learn typing and shorthand for some kind of writing. The risks of returning to detecting were considerable: of the 914 TB patients discharged from the San Francisco Tuberculosis Hospital from 1918 to 1921, according to a report, some 247 of them died after attempting to "resume their normal occupations before they had gained sufficient strength."[1]

The Flood Building was a twelve-story, sandstone-faced structure downtown on Market Street, beside the cable car turntable on Powell. An appealingly solid survivor of the earthquake and fire, its offices followed a central oblong courtyard.

In room 314, Pinkerton's made an exotic presence among the building's dental and medical tenants. If you walk the Flood's marble hallways today, long after the agency's departure, the clatter of stone underfoot and the sunlit frosted glass of each office doorway evoke films from the Sam Spade era. Hammett's time as a working sleuth in San Francisco may have been no more than six or eight vivid months, due to the cycles of his illness, but in these halls he formed our idea of what a private detective's office should look like.

The branch manager was Phil Geauque (pronounced JEE-ack), Hammett's final boss as a Pinkerton. Unlike "Jimmy Wright," the name Hammett gave for his first supervisor in Baltimore, Geauque undeniably existed, turning up in the press from time to time and going on to a later career with the U.S. Secret Service.* Short, fortyish, balding, and a heavy smoker, he was not a desk type but kept a hand in working the field. Physically he resembled Hammett's Continental Op and had many experiences worthy of detective fiction: The con man who staged a car wreck, and then faked amnesia in order to hide from police inside a Stockton asylum. Or the Yellow Cab

---

* As a Secret Service agent, Geauque once pursued a passerby he saw carrying a small piece of counterfeiting equipment into a residence. His eagerness to follow resulted in the case *Poldo v. United States* (1932), which held that he had made an unauthorized, if successful, search of a suspect's premises. A founder of the International Footprinters' Society, he lectured in later years on counterfeiting detection techniques. The mistaken claim that he later guarded President Franklin Roosevelt stems, I think, from a misunderstanding of what the Secret Service primarily does—fight counterfeiting. In the forties, he frequently spoke to civic groups, introducing a cautionary Secret Service film called *Know Your Money.*

cashier who filched twenty-two thousand dollars in Chicago, and then increased it gambling his way to the El Paso boardinghouse where he was arrested. Or the Menlo Park family taken hostage by liquor thieves stealing dozens of cases of the estate's collection; a neighbor was finally alerted when a nanny tossed a note from an upstairs window.[2]

Discussing these days in later years, Hammett packed an impressive caseload into his months as an operative in San Francisco. Some of the jobs, such as working the docks for the strikebreaker Blackjack Jerome or climbing a smokestack to search for missing gold, seem physically ambitious feats for a tubercular man whose weight fluctuated during this time between 132 and 126 pounds,[3] nearly 20 pounds below his healthy weight. He was especially too weak for this kind of work on first arrival in San Francisco, when the army judged him 100 percent disabled.

But the versions he spun for interviewers bore the hallmarks of his splendid storytelling, what the Ellery Queen writer Frederic Dannay called the "skin of realism," which helped sell them. His claim of going undercover in the San Francisco jail, emerging only with a case of lice, may or may not be true, but it certainly has a grubby plausibility; his story of being hospitalized for months as a Pinkerton befriending a suspect in an adjoining bed, however, is less likely than that he was simply bedridden for one of his TB attacks. But even the half-experiences he had had as a Pinkerton he later learned to parlay vividly in stories and interviews, a method described best by his own Continental Op in "Zigzags of Treachery":

> I talked about myself with the evasiveness that would have been natural to a crook in my situation; and made one or two

carefully planned slips that would lead him to believe that I had been tied up with the "Jimmy the Riveter" hold-up mob, most of whom were doing long hitches at Walla Walla then.

The Jimmy the Riveter mob was in fact apprehended by the Pinkertons near Seattle in the fall of 1921, during Hammett's last months on the job. It's possible he was even there, despite his bad health and the impending birth of his first child, Mary, who arrived on October 16, since it made enough of an impression on him that he later traced two of his characters to the gang (Babe McCloor and Hymie the Riveter). But he didn't have to be a witness to exploit an incident for his writing, as he did with his account of staking out the Minnesota jewel thief Gloomy Gus Schaefer in Vallejo, California in 1921: "While trying to peer into the upper story of a roadhouse in northern California one night—and the man I was looking for was in Seattle at the time—part of the porch roof crumbled under me and I fell, spraining an ankle. The proprietor of the roadhouse gave me water to bathe it in."

He's not claiming he caught him, just that he watched his house, which fell down. That's good storytelling, whether it happened or not. The anecdotes he fed to reporters can feel like "carefully planned slips" by the ex-detective. "This is what you wanted to hear, wasn't it?" he asked the *Brooklyn Eagle*'s Helen Herbert Foster in 1929. "All reporters want to hear such experiences from detectives. And these are authentic enough, goodness knows."

★　★　★

BY THE EARLY 1970s, sadly little proof remained of Hammett's employment as a Pinkerton beyond the word of his family.

David Fechheimer would change that. While working out of the very same Pinkerton branch, he had become increasingly interested in the history of the man whom no one at the businesslike Flood Building seemed to remember.

When people meet Fechheimer today, his stealthy profession doesn't seem at first to jibe with his trim white beard and rimless glasses, which might suggest a professor of American studies, perhaps, or constitutional law, instead of a detective. When he arrived in San Francisco in the early sixties, it was still "Hammett's city. Men wore hats, everybody drank."[4] But by 1965 the city was entering its countercultural bloom; Fechheimer was a "budding flower child" and poet on his way to a literature degree at San Francisco State when he encountered the books that got him off his academic track.

"We all lived hand-to-mouth then," he says, and all were looking for work; after admiring the collection of Hammett's other jobs listed on the backs of his novels, Fechheimer called up Pinkerton's San Francisco branch and began his own detecting career where the writer had finished his. He learned all the skills of sleuthing and, later, under his longtime boss Hal Lipset, quite a few tricks unknown to Hammett, before eventually going into practice himself as a San Francisco private eye. Like Hammett, he began to learn the city around him right down to its bones.

As an investigator, Fechheimer noticed things: While waiting for the M car on the traffic island opposite the House of Lucky Wedding Rings, he met Albert Samuels Jr. who was out sweeping the sidewalk and whose father had once employed Hammett to write jewelry ads. Fechheimer got his hair cut by an old barber named Bill Sibilia, who remembered trimming

Hammett's graying pompadour and that he was a good tipper. Fechheimer also located a woman Hammett had written poems for in San Francisco; she talked to him in whispers outside her house, having never told her husband about her admirer. He next found and interviewed Mrs. Hammett, long presumed dead by scholars at the time. Then, hoping to find any of his hero's old colleagues, he used the same method that had drawn Hammett into the agency to begin with: he placed a simple newspaper ad.

Two old men answered his query: Jack Knight had been a well-traveled Pinkerton in the early twenties who never worked directly with Hammett but who knew of his reputation as one of the "fellows with particular ability." The other, Phil Haultain, said he had learned to shadow from "Sam" Hammett himself, and was his partner in the last months of Hammett's career as an operative. Fechheimer went to meet Haultain in the office of his conveyor belt company in Emeryville, California, in early September 1975. Their conversation remains the only eyewitness testimony about Hammett as a detective.[5]

Shaking the old operative's hand, Fechheimer must have felt, in the words of A. J. Liebling, "joined onto the past like a man's arm to his shoulder." Haultain, at eighty years old, looked paunchy but stockily powerful at his desk. He wore a buff-colored Stetson, dark plaid shirt, flower-pattern tie, and thin white mustache. "I was telling my wife today," he said, "Sam Hammett made me a good shadow man." Haultain recalled his Pinkerton mentor as "tall, thin, smart as a steel trap. He knew his business. He wasn't a drinking man in those days, not that I know of. But he used to smoke like hell. Rolled his own cigarettes." Their supervisor, Phil Geauque, was "an exciting guy to work for. He was sharp, and I think that's probably why he liked Hammett."*

According to Haultain, Hammett schooled him in shadowing that fall of 1921, when Pinkerton's was hired by the defense in the first manslaughter trial of the film comedian Roscoe "Fatty" Arbuckle. The two men were tailing a couple from Los Angeles who were likely witnesses for the prosecution, and Haultain remembered "we circled round them, and even with this hat [of mine], they didn't get wise. He was a wonderful investigator."

They were tailing potential witnesses because of what had happened at the St. Francis Hotel on September 5, 1921, when a wild Labor Day party took over three suites on that hotel's top floor. The partiers had traveled from Hollywood to honor the star of *The Butcher Boy*, *Crazy to Marry*, and *Good Night, Nurse*, Fatty Arbuckle, who had recently signed a new million-dollar studio contract. The Arbuckle group had come to the wide-open "City That Knows How" for a bash featuring plenty of bathtub gin, but the party, reported in newspapers to have been like a Roman orgy, turned as disastrous as it was debauched, leaving one woman dead and Arbuckle accused.

Far from the funny man the public knew, Arbuckle suddenly became a rapacious symbol of dark Hollywood; in forcing himself on a young actress and party girl named Virginia Rappe,

---

* Haultain also showed Fechheimer an antique novelty on his desk: a darkened, decorated human head opened at the top like a half coconut shell. He claimed to have shown Hammett the object in the early twenties and wondered aloud if it might later have stoked Hammett's imagination while he was writing *The Maltese Falcon*.

he had, prosecutors claimed, crushed her beneath his 260-pound body and ruptured her bladder. (She died several days later, in another room of the hotel.) Other theories explaining Rappe's death—that she was suffering from the clap or was injured from a recent illegal abortion—could not compete with the more sensational charges made by an alleged witness, an older woman who swore she had seen Arbuckle emerge from the crime scene room in his pajamas; her background as a madam and extortionist kept her off the stand but not out of the papers.

If he had appeared in a Hammett story, Arbuckle would probably have been villainous, too, like a number of the writer's sinister hefty characters, culminating in *The Maltese Falcon*'s Casper Gutman, with his "bulbous pink cheeks and chins and neck" and "great soft egg of a belly . . . and pendant cones for arms and legs." Hammett felt instead that Arbuckle had been the victim of a "frame-up" by a careerist district attorney and a fervent gang of newsmen. As he set it down in an unpublished piece:

> I sat in the lobby of the Plaza, in San Francisco. It was the day before the opening of the second absurd attempt to convict Roscoe Arbuckle of something. He came into the lobby. He looked at me and I at him. His eyes were the eyes of a man who expected to be regarded as a monster but was not yet inured to it. I made my gaze as contemptuous as I could. He glared at me, went on to the elevator still glaring. It was amusing. I was working for his attorneys at the time, gathering information for his defence.[6]

It is unlikely that Hammett headed up the Arbuckle investigation, as some writers have argued, but the case was big enough for Pinkerton's that most hands would have been pressed into service. Even though his wife did not recall his working on it, if Hammett was well enough to get out of bed, then, based on Haultain's remembrance, it is believable that he was sufficiently involved to have knowledge of the case, if not enough to brag about it to his wife. But by December 1921, days after the first Arbuckle trial ended with a 10–2 vote to acquit,* Hammett's TB was back; the army restored his 100 percent disability. This latest crash could have been brought on by all the shadow work, the smoking, climbing, and the cold morning fog.

Was the Arbuckle case Sam Hammett's last? Sometimes it was, but more often he claimed the *Sonoma* gold theft as his swan song. After considerable study in the 1970s, the mystery author Joe Gores called the *Sonoma* job "Hammett's final investigation as a Pinkerton operative." It certainly offered him a more poetic exit: solving a crime too quickly for his own good. It was a perfect self-deprecating end to his detecting life. Asked in 1934 why he had finally left his career with Pinkerton's, Hammett answered, "I suppose because they wouldn't let me go to Australia after some stolen gold. It sounded romantic."

On November 23, 1921, the steamship SS *Sonoma* returned to San Francisco by way of Sydney, Auckland, Pago Pago, and Honolulu. Along with its bags of far-flung mail, the ship carried $375,000 worth of English gold specie. The gold had come

---

* It was declared a mistrial, and Arbuckle was tried two more times before he was unanimously acquitted in April 1922, far too late to save even the scraps of his career. He never starred in another film.

aboard under bank supervision one half hour before the ship left Sydney, and had been undisturbed for the rest of the voyage, according to the crew, locked away in the ship's strong room. When officials arrived to unload it in San Francisco, however, they noticed that one of the three strong room locks had been switched and no longer opened with the captain's key, while inside, some $125,000 worth of gold was missing. The ship was impounded at the pier, and detectives were called in.

Although by this time he was strong enough to venture out for only a few hours at a time, Hammett could have answered the call for operatives to go down to the bulkhead wharf building at Pier 35 while the ship's crew and passengers were being investigated, especially as the search went on for several days.

The way Lillian Hellman remembered Hammett telling it:

[He] and another operative met the boat as it docked, examined all sailors and officers, searched the boat, but couldn't find the gold. They knew the gold had to be on the boat, and so the agency decided that when the boat sailed home Hammett should sail with it.[7]

Hammett excitedly packed his bags, and then "the head of the agency suggested they give a last, hopeless search. Hammett climbed a smokestack he had examined several times before, looked down and shouted, 'They moved it. It's here.'" Scolding himself for not finding the loot once they were at least out to sea, "He fished out the gold, took it back to the Pinkerton office, and resigned that afternoon." The self-rebuke makes his heroism less flashy, but it is still not likely that this tubercular part-time detective would clamber up a smokestack, let alone do it more than once.

In fact, the gold was not even found by a Pinkerton. While knocking on some pipes, crewmember Carl Knudsen discovered $29,000 of it stuffed inside a fire hose that had been lowered into the *Sonoma*'s chimney, while police detectives found $75,000 more hanging from buoy markers beneath the pier. Newspapers tried to sell an account that the gold's hiding place visited First Assistant Engineer Knudsen in a dream, but Knudsen denied it, and Hammett's later version makes a much better story.

You don't have to believe Hammett solved the theft to grant that he could have done just enough legwork around the docks to later write about it memorably, giving the *Sonoma* a cameo in *The Maltese Falcon* (as *La Paloma*). Also, the gold was discovered on November 28, and Hammett was again judged 100 percent disabled in early December. Although he always needed money, the only reason to think he did any detective work after this is the word of his Pinkerton colleague Phil Haultain.

★   ★   ★

"I REMEMBER THIS one time, we were working on the hold-up of the California Street Cable Company," recalled Phil Haultain decades later. "And Sam said, 'You'd better take a gun. No, you'd better take two.'"[8]

This statement turns out to have the hard-boiled air of truth, as even their own supervisor, Phil Geauque, would fire his weapon in the field that day. Because of the testimony of his young partner and the fact that his boss was seen mixing it up, it seems reasonable that Hammett could have been on the job, too. And yet, on paper he should have been largely bed-ridden by this time.*

TWO YOUNG MEN had boarded the cable car just before noon on January 3, 1922, hailing it opposite the car barn at Hyde and California Streets and riding on as it climbed the steepening grade in the winter sunlight. One of them claimed the rear platform of the car, near the gripman, while the other took the front, beside the conductor. Among the pack of thirty or forty passengers inside sat two officials from the California Cable Car Company, who had boarded along with the men and were accompanying a leather pouch filled with three-days' sales receipts on their way to the bank.

When the car reached Jones Street, two more strangers came on, taking their place on the front and rear platforms. The group of four then drew guns on the gripman and conductor and took command of the car from both ends as it continued along California Street. They next closed on the pair of cable car executives with the money bag in the center of the car, adding fifty dollars to the take from the pocket of assistant cashier Boger; at the far corner of Jones Street, the four holdup men jumped off, carrying the leather bag and its $3,550. They climbed into an open automobile whose driver, Samuel Salter, an auto mechanic from an Ellis Street garage, had been hired to tour San Francisco after their original taxi broke down. Salter

---

* When I asked David Fechheimer what else he remembered from his 1975 interview with Phil Haultain, whether Hammett could have meant "Let's each of us take two" guns or "I can't go with you, so you'd better take two," he noted that the quote works either way.

was told cryptically to wait a few minutes. After his passengers leapt off the cable car carrying a leather pouch, one got in beside him and trained a revolver on Salter and shouted, "Take your hand off that brake and let's see you go." Salter drove crazily downhill—very much like a man with a gun to his head—to Pine Street, where one of the gang jumped from the car, his split somehow already divided out. The gang left their driver at the entrance to Golden Gate Park. He drove straight to the Hall of Justice to tell his story, but shotgun squads could find no sign of the gang.

Days later, detectives went to the house of a man named Frank Grider in San Francisco. They wanted to interview him about his son Frank Jr., who was suspected in the cable car robbery and had turned up in Salt Lake City. Two extra Pinkertons, G. A. Robinson and Hammett's supervisor, Phil Geauque, were standing outside the elder Grider's home when another son, the suspect's sixteen-year-old brother, Edwin Grider, appeared. Edwin saw that his father's house was lively with detectives and bolted. Robinson and Geauque called halt, fired a volley after him, and then grabbed the boy as he was climbing into a taxi.[9]

His partner's memory and their supervisor's public involvement in the case suggest that Hammett worked the cable car robbery a little and heard about the rest in the office and from the newspaper accounts. Or perhaps, since he was supposedly bedridden during this time, he told Phil Haultain to "take two" guns with him that day because Hammett himself couldn't accompany him. If Haultain is to be believed, and Hammett was somehow able to work even a piece of the case, then this would certainly have been his last investigation. As he began courses at Munson's School of Stenography and Typing to prepare to be some kind of reporter, Hammett resigned from Pinkerton's in February 1922, weeks after the robbery. Since arriving in San Francisco, he had been periodically examined by a visiting nurse at his Eddy Street apartment to verify his claims of disability. But on February 15 he somehow got himself to the Flood Building for an exam in the Pinkerton office. It's unclear why it took place there, but the appointment does prove that even when sick he could will himself to work. Whether or not he formally resigned that day, it is the last date that Hammett is known to have been in the Pinkerton offices.

By this time, Hammett's weight was again as low as when he was sent home from the army.[10] His retirement from detecting was actually a quieter departure than the resignation on principle over the *Sonoma* case reported by Lillian Hellman. He may have told better stories to Hellman over the years, but the unglamorous truth behind his quitting was well known to Josephine Hammett. As she later told David Fechheimer when he found her in Los Angeles, her husband "stopped 'cause he took sick. He couldn't do that stuff anymore. You know, go out in the fog."[11]

Part II

THE EX-DETECTIVE

I decided to become a writer. It was a good idea.
Having had no experience whatever in writing, except
writing letters and reports, I wasn't handicapped by
exaggerated notions of the difficulties ahead.

—DASHIELL HAMMETT, 1929

Chapter VII

A LITTLE MAN GOING FORWARD

*I'm not what you'd call a brilliant thinker—such results
as I get are usually the fruits of patience, industry, and
unimaginative plugging, helped out now and then,
maybe, by a little luck—but I do have my flashes of
intelligence.*

—"Zigzags of Treachery" (1924)

O N   A   D A Y   in late June 1922, William A. Pinkerton, surviving son of the founder and himself the most famous
detective in the world, was visiting San Francisco to attend an
international convention of police chiefs, a favorite annual event
in a city he called his spiritual home. The detective was now past
seventy-five, a large, dapper man whose wide, soft hat echoed his
younger days chasing Western train robbers. During his week
in California he hoped to hear about the latest techniques in
crime fighting, to dine with old lawman friends, and to hold forth
about the uses of intelligence as the head of Pinkerton's National
Detective Agency.[1]

Pinkerton had checked into the St. Francis Hotel, facing

Union Square, where he had stayed happily and eventfully on other visits from Chicago. He had once received a note in the hotel's dining room inviting him to what he guessed would be an attempt on his life; Pinkerton kept the appointment, and at his signal of slyly touching his hat, detectives grabbed the assassin before he could fire.

While trying to take a walk in the springtime air, Pinkerton was approached by a reporter from the *San Francisco Chronicle*, who asked if the old detective had time for a question. Pinkerton agreed, and the two men returned to his room, where he removed his hat from his center-parted gray head and bore down on his interviewer with his dark eyes.

"Shoot," he said.

The *Chronicle*'s man could have asked any number of questions to ensure a more colorful interview. Speaking at a previous year's conference, for instance, Pinkerton had made news by disparaging the work of U.S. Army Intelligence against the "radical" threat. The reporter might have also asked about the agency's relentless manhunt that dismantled Butch Cassidy's Hole-in-the-Wall gang and chased Butch himself to South America; or about Pinkerton's youthful wounding by a train robber, Hilary Farrington, whose struggle with Pinkerton aboard a paddlewheeler ended with Farrington going over the side to his death. He might have asked about Pinkerton's more recent call for a return to the whipping post or about the Agency's work the previous year on Fatty Arbuckle's manslaughter trial, which stemmed from events at this same hotel.

Instead, the reporter threw something soft and slow: "What do you think of detective stories?"

"They're the bunk—rot," roared the old man, prompting a follow-up: "Have you ever read a detective story that read like the person who wrote it knew what he was talking about?"

The renowned old sleuth, whose Scottish father had founded the country's first detective agency, sniffed at the suggestion. "Never. And I don't expect to." He especially panned the Sherlock Holmes tales of Arthur Conan Doyle. "These stories about detectives tracing crime by scratches on the back of watches and all that sort of rot give the people the wrong idea about the way we work. Detective work is only using good, common sense—nothing else," Pinkerton said. "Any man with good common sense can be a detective. I've picked some of my men from street cars and all sorts of occupations, and they have usually made good."[2]

That summer of 1922, when William Pinkerton sermonized the reporter, Sam Hammett had been making small steps toward assembling a career as an ex-detective. Since the birth of his daughter in October 1921, he had been sleeping alone, as advised due to his TB, in a Murphy bed in the hallway of their Eddy Street apartment, to keep safely apart from the baby. The family had been kept out of total poverty by a small, grudging loan made by his father. The fact that Hammett would even overrule his pride to ask such a favor of Richard Hammett shows how desperate things had become. While often kept home by his health, since February he had also been taking secretarial courses at the Munson School on Sutter Street. In addition to learning how to take quick notes, he was mastering touch typing, with which he turned out both the stories and poems he sent to magazines and the meticulous letters of outrage he wrote to the Veterans' Bureau about changes to his pension. He kept writing, when he could, at a table in the kitchen and sometimes in the big sunny reading room at the public library.

Reporting would eventually have presented some of the same physical challenges as detective work as he ran down stories.[3] He needed work he could do at home—or, when at his worst, even flat on his back. Though bedridden much of each day, Hammett somehow continued to combine hustle with the understandably fatal view that TB would someday finish him off. "He would have done whatever he had to do to make a buck," says David Fechheimer. "He was never a very good invalid."* He had to come up with a less physically taxing way of making money.

Without any surviving manuscripts before he was in his late twenties, it is hard to date exactly his decision to become a writer, let alone what kind of writer he wanted to be. He may not have respected the mystery story as it was then practiced, but he did not set out to reinvent it, either. His first attempts at writing actually were short, droll pieces, allegories, poems, character sketches, and what he called "legit" fiction, a form he never gave up the dream of returning to even after the success of his crime stories. His early efforts were more literary than "hard-boiled," a recent term for skill under fire popularized by the ghastly war.

That spring of 1922, at the age of twenty-eight, he typed up a draft of his first short story, "The Barber and His Wife," on

---

* To further cloud the issue of his employment, Hammett listed himself in the 1923 City Directory as "broker," a possible lingering cover for sleuthing work.

his new black Underwood at the kitchen table. The story features a brawny, well-dressed husband and his unsatisfied wife to whom he gives hardly a thought; a brother with recognizable lung trouble; and a cultured young man who takes the wife to the movies. It reads a bit like a lesser Sherwood Anderson story until a coolly observed scene of violence when the husband visits the young suitor's office:

> He stopped before Becker's desk and the younger man looked up at Louis through pale, harassed eyes.
> "Is this Mr. Becker?"
> "Yes, sir. Won't you have a seat?"
> "No," Louis said evenly, "what I'm going to say ought to be said standing up." He appreciated the bewilderment in the salesman's eyes. "I'm Louis Stemler!"

His debut story was rejected before finally finding a home that fall, but in June or July of 1922, Hammett had his first sale of a sardonic parable of fewer than a hundred words called "The Parthian Shot," bought for *The Smart Set* by its famous editor H. L. Mencken, the most celebrated graduate of the school Hammett had attended through eighth grade, Baltimore Polytechnic. It was impressive for anyone to receive a letter from the great Mencken, but especially thrilling if you had grown up living in Baltimore, where he was the godlike driving force at the *Sun*. This first sale did not go far toward paying the Hammetts' bills, but it allowed the struggling family to do something comparatively lavish—to order in dinner to celebrate. The little dinner must have been a highlight of that summer in which Hammett's mother died, on August 3, 1922.

His first crime story, "The Road Home," was bought by a magazine of a lower rank, *The Black Mask*, which ran it that December of 1922. Mencken and George Jean Nathan had founded this magazine just two years earlier as one of several vehicles for funding their true love, the more rarefied *Smart Set*. (These fund-raising vehicles included an erotic sampler, *Saucy Stories*, and something called the *Parisienne*.) When *The Black Mask* debuted in 1920, crime and detection were only a part of the splashy mix that also featured adventure, romance, cowboys, mystery, and occult. Mencken, despite his love of street slang as a brilliant chronicler of the American language, did not publicize his connection to *The Black Mask* and kept his name off the masthead altogether, and he and Nathan sold the magazine after its first eight issues.

Likewise, Hammett kept his own name off his debut in *The Black Mask*, using the pseudonym Peter Collinson, and allegedly saving his real name for poetry.* But if he saw publishing in *The Black Mask* as slumming it, he certainly got over this view with time, writing mostly for lower-paying crime magazines by the mid-twenties.

"The Road Home" had no tricks or acts of genius in its detection, but an American view of crime acquired by the writer as a Pinkerton: A lean "manhunter" named Hagedorn has spent two years tracking his subject to a jungly corner of

---

* "Peter Collins" was an old carnival term for "Nobody" that Hammett might have learned as an operative. "Peter Collinson" therefore meant "Son of Nobody." In publishing this first detective story, he might also have feared repercussions from the Agency, although he also used the "Collinson" byline for such harmless early efforts as "The Sardonic Star of Tom Doody."

Burma. Hagedorn intends to bring back his prisoner to New York, but Barnes, who's claimed a local gem bed worth a criminal fortune, offers Hagedorn a piece of his kingdom if he'll return home with false proof of the crook's death. Instead of the detective following clues to snare his man, Hammett begins mid-showdown on a river, Barnes shouting out his bribe offer and Hagedorn quietly considering the criminal's invitation to take his share of the gems. Barnes escapes ashore, forcing the issue; Hagedorn hesitates, then follows him into the trees, saying, "Oh, hell! It may take five years. I wonder about them jewels of his." It's left unclear whether Hagedorn will do the right thing or even survive his trek into the jungle, a challenge to the pieties of the detective story. "The puzzle isn't so interesting to me as the behavior of the detective attacking it," Hammett would say.

"The Road Home" is flavored with words that its author, who had never been overseas, clearly dug out of the public library (*muggar, Mran-ma, jahaz*), but the premise derives from his firsthand knowledge of Pinkerton work: The situation resembles a less exotic story Hammett liked to tell of himself, of shadowing a suspicious jewel salesman named Finsterwald from Philadelphia to Savannah, only to have the thief finally approach him in a public park as looking vaguely "familiar" and offer him a share of his swindle. (Hammett turned him in.) This proposition was dramatically interesting, especially if the reader was left unsure of the detective's answer, a daring step into the jungle for this kind of fiction.

A writer without Hammett's work experience might have shied away from a two-year manhunt overseas as too bold a plot to be believed. But Hammett would have heard plenty such tales around the detectives' room: William R. Sayers's two years spent chasing a man through Europe were hardly the toughest part of a career in which he also rode with the Pinkerton crew that ran down the Wild Bunch gang. (And William Pinkerton himself had worked months in London and Havana to bring back the brilliant English forger Austin Bidwell.)[4]

Hammett continued to cover all his bases as a struggling freelancer, sending out an ambitious range of apprentice work—poems, essays, sketches. It is probable, though, as the writer Vince Emery suggests, that his researches in the public library led him to create a series character, inspired both by his irritation with the hackneyed detective fiction he saw in the pulps and on the theory that stories with a known character would eventually command a better price.

His next crime story, "Arson Plus," had a striding confidence that his other work lacked, from its opening sentence in which a detective rolls a cigar across the desk of a fat small-town sheriff to earn his cooperation. The story introduced a savvy little hero whose adventures allowed Hammett to exploit both his detecting experiences and growing knowledge of San Francisco. His narrator was unnamed but spoke in the style of the classic op reports, tracing his days and nights of methodical plugging—interviewing comely nieces and elderly house servants, matching alibis against hotel registers, visiting a dead man's grocer, and even checking his final laundry ticket. Of all the available ways to write about detecting since Edgar Allan Poe's Parisian investigator C. Auguste Dupin first appeared in 1841 in "The Murders in the Rue Morgue," Hammett opted to do something that grew out of what he had actually been trained for: creating elevated stories from the characters and situations he knew well, instead of adding to the fiction club of gentleman puzzlers or quick-draw artists. This approach would eventually set crime writing on its head.

★ ★ ★

HAMMETT'S NAMELESS OP first appeared in October 1923, when *The Black Mask* published "Arson Plus" (again by "Peter Collinson"). Its narrator resembles many of the operatives whose dispatches are collected in the Pinkerton archives at the Library of Congress, only unlike most of the standard op reports Hammett knew well, "Arson Plus" begins to make literature out of the tedium of investigation:

> Having ruined our shoe-shines, McClump and I got back in our machine and swung off in a circle around the place, calling at all the houses within a mile radius, and getting little besides jolts for our trouble.

A skinny near-convalescent writing about his little man of action, Hammett had created a streetwise yet incorruptible hero who is devoted to the job at hand, however unsavory the client, a code Hammett had absorbed from Pinkerton's:

"Next morning, at the address McClump had given me—a rather elaborate apartment building on California Street—I had to wait three-quarters of an hour for Mrs. Evelyn Trowbridge to dress." In ordinary circumstances, Mrs. Trowbridge's appearance would have made it well worth the wait, explains the Op, "But I was a busy, middle-aged detective, who was fuming over having his time wasted; and I was a lot more interested in finding the bird who struck the match than I was in feminine beauty. However, I smothered my grouch, apologized for disturbing her at such an early hour, and got down to business." The detective must smother all kinds of distracting feelings to keep his eye on the job.

These lines mark one of many times Hammett's Op declines to name himself—though he does describe himself as portly, around forty, and five foot six—while slogging his way through twenty-six stories, two linked novellas, and two full-length novels.

In May of that year, *The Black Mask* had published the first story about a "tough guy" private investigator, Terry Mack. Chronologically, Carroll John Daly's "Three Gun Terry" ran weeks ahead of Hammett's debut of his Continental Op that fall. But beyond being set inside a detective's office, the two stories had very little in common. Daly's "Three Gun" Terry character was the flashy, sharpshooting opposite of the Op, while another of Daly's heroes, Race Williams, debuted in the June 1 issue in a timely story about an investigation of the Ku Klux Klan, "Knights of the Open Palm." It was just the kind of thing Hammett was trying to correct in detective fiction, unrealistic action delivered in an unconvincing vernacular: "I'm what you might call a middleman—just a halfway house between the dicks and the crooks. Oh, there ain't no doubt that both the cops and the crooks take me for a gun, but I ain't—not rightly speaking."[5]

By comparison, Hammett's Op had wrung some handy knowledge from his rough life of sleuthing: Abductions rarely occur at night or in cities, and those that do more likely are staged by the victim for ransom; no one can strangle you from the front if your arms are free to reach up and snap his pinkies; when a "Chinese" starts shooting, he always empties his gun;

you can shadow anyone pretty naturally if you don't meet the subject's eye; it's best to stand aside of the door during "unannounced" visits in case bullets burst through it; even a light tap to the head with a metal revolver has a surprisingly concussive effect; you can often draw good information or even a confession "out of a feeble nature" by putting your face close to the subject's and talking loudly; people talk more freely in a room with a closed door; and any hop head who tells you his name is "John Ryan" is not to be trusted ("it's the John Smith of yeggdom").

Hammett's Op is suspicious of brilliance and puts his faith in doing the basic parts of his job well and hoping for occasional "flashes of intelligence." Though he is hard or congenial as the situation requires, this "little block of a man" sometimes surprises himself with what he'll do for the job, such as shooting a woman criminal in the leg who had gambled that gallantry would leave him unable to fire as she fled. ("I had never shot a woman before. I felt queer about it.") If he goes home, he is often interrupted while changing into his pajamas or is jangled awake by a call from his chilly master at the agency, known only as the Old Man. The Op knows his crooks, and strikes the balance of criminal expertise, anonymity, and loyalty to the client that Allan Pinkerton had prescribed.

The idea that he was modeled on a particular Pinkerton drawn from life comes mainly from Hammett, as relayed by one half of the writing team of Ellery Queen, Frederic Dannay, who later edited a number of Hammett paperback collections. Sometime in the late thirties, Dannay had dined with Hammett at Lüchow's, the cavernous, celebrated German restaurant on Fourteenth Street in New York City known for its house band

and beer garden specialties.[6] After talking about many subjects and sampling "various liquids ranging from pale yellow to dark brown," Dannay remembered, the "amber fluids" at last loosened Hammett's tongue and he gave up "the lowdown" about his character. The Op was based "on a real-life person— James (Jimmy) Wright, Assistant Superintendent, in the good old days, of Pinkerton's Baltimore agency, under whom Dashiell Hammett actually worked."[7]

The key to this story might be the amber fluids drunk by the diners and a bit of detective's whimsy on Hammett's part, since the name he cited went back decades as a Pinkerton alias. As explained earlier, the existence of a genuine Jimmy Wright is difficult to confirm. If anyone, the Op better resembles Hammett's real San Francisco boss Phil Geauque, still working as an active Secret Service agent in the thirties. It's most likely, though, that the Op was a composite or "type," as Hammett described his character in 1929:

> I've worked with half a dozen men who might be he with few changes. Though he may be "different" in fiction, he is almost pure "type" in life. I've always tried to hold him as close to the "type" as possible because what I see in him is a little man going forward day after day through mud and blood and death and deceit—as callous and brutal and cynical as is necessary—towards a dim goal, with nothing to push or pull him towards it except that he'd been hired to reach it—a sort of Manuel whose saying is: "The job's got to be done."[8]

All Pinkertons signed an agreement against disclosure, and the fate of the cowboy detective Charlie Siringo had shown that even the most sanitized detective memoir could be punished by the Pinkertons. So Hammett had to create his own mythical agency, as lawyers had forced poor Siringo to do. A fan of inside jokes to amuse himself, Hammett named the firm that employed his Op the Continental Detective Agency, after the Continental Building in Baltimore, where he had first been hired by Pinkerton's, and he gave it a location that is clearly modeled on the Flood Building in San Francisco. A later story in *True Detective* magazine was even credited "By Dashiell Hammett of the Continental Detective Agency." In a sense, Hammett worked there the rest of his life.

Following "Arson Plus," a second Op story, "Slippery Fingers," ran in the October 15 issue of *The Black Mask*, also attributed to "Peter Collinson." "Slippery Fingers" does not rank with Hammett's best, but it is significant for another reason. The murderer in the tale schemes with an expert to make counterfeit gelatin fingerprints, which he wears after leaving his real bloody prints all over the death scene. This kind of forgery seemed plausible to many in 1923, as the criminal science of fingerprint identification was taking hold with the public, but not to Berkeley's police chief August Vollmer, a champion of fingerprint identification and of the emerging lie detector technology. Vollmer was a highly successful and gentlemanly crime fighter with a national reputation, recently elected president of the International Organization of Chiefs of Police, whose new techniques William Pinkerton himself had approved the year before.

Transferring genuine prints from one crime scene to another might be possible, Vollmer told the *Chronicle* that fall, but "Close inspection of any forged finger-print will soon cause detection." This was alarming news to the young author of a new story featuring such forgery. Clearly worried over possible challenges to his story and his knowledge as an ex-detective, Hammett wrote to the editor at *The Black Mask*:

> It may be that what Farr does in my story would be considered by Mr. Vollmer a transference rather than a forgery. But whichever it is, I think there is no longer reasonable room for doubt that fingerprints can be successfully forged. I have seen forged prints that to me seemed perfect, but, not being even an amateur in that line, my opinion isn't worth much.[9]

Hammett contradicts the only expert he has named, August Vollmer,* and then concludes that "quite a number of those qualified to speak on the subject will agree with me," and while claiming to have seen forged prints, he admits he would be unable to recognize them, a shrewd dodge. Both *The Black Mask* and a competitor, *Detective Story Magazine*, had started their own fingerprint departments the year before, and Hammett may have particularly feared a challenge to his forensics knowledge from a house specialist. "I found I could sell the stories easily when it became known I had been a Pinkerton man," he remembered. "People thought my stuff was authentic." This letter is a rare example of Hammett

---

* Despite his pronouncements on the subject, Vollmer was pranked himself by one of his Berkeley officers, who claimed to have successfully transferred Vollmer's own prints to a crime scene, stoking the debate about fingerprint forgery/transference and outraging his boss.

defending his authenticity, which was so important to the reception of what he wrote and the writer he became.

Having now published at the high and lower ends of the magazine spectrum, he brought his worldly detective voice to the cultured readers of *The Smart Set*, where he had broken in with his short, droll "The Parthian Shot" the year before and published two other sketches since. "From the Memoirs of a Private Detective," a deadpan teaser of twenty-nine authentic-sounding snippets and scenes from his former profession, appeared in the March 1923 issue. In it, he carefully never mentioned Pinkerton's National Detective Agency but wrote as "Dashiell Hammett" in the role he would play the rest of his life, of the literate ex-detective.

He began:

Wishing to get some information from some members of the W.C.T.U. in an Oregon city, I introduced myself as the secretary of the Butte Civic Purity League. One of them read me a long discourse on the erotic effects of cigarettes on young girls. Subsequent experiments proved this tip worthless.

Hammett knew the *Smart Set* audience well. Aiming to entertain but not offend, he recalled nothing as ugly as strikebreaking, but his selections highlighted the kind of quirky jobs Pinkerton's might have asked of its operatives, without naming the agency or its clients—discharging a woman's housekeeper for her; circulating among unimpressive forgers, pickpockets, and embezzlers scattered among cities and countryside. Most house burglars "live on their women," he observed, while "Of all the men embezzling from their employers with whom I have had contact, I can't remember a dozen who smoked, drank, or had any of the vices in which bonding companies are so interested." A forger he knew left his wife because she had learned to smoke cigarettes while he was in prison. As biography, "Memoirs" is sadly slim, but anything more specific might have been unpublishable, drawing the quick wrath of Pinkerton's, and wouldn't have fit *Smart Set*'s high tone.

True or even partially true, these tales certainly went down more easily the way Hammett told them, but there was a limit. "I once knew a man who stole a Ferris wheel," he reported, a claim for only the truest believers. (A decade later he would add that he had found the giant stolen ride at a competing amusement park and resented reports since made that he had "stolen" it himself, as if rescuing the enormous wheel were more believable than stealing it.)

"I was a pretty good sleuth," Hammett boasted in 1929, "but a bit overrated because of the plausibility with which I could explain away my failures, proving them inevitable and no fault of mine." In fact, plausibility would be a key part of his art.

While his first writing sales were a boost to his spirits, they did not add up to a living. As a satirist or poet he might not have distinguished himself from the pack, but the credibly gritty feel of his crime writings was already setting them apart from the more lurid and fanciful stuff found in detective magazines.

Chapter VIII

THE OLD MAN

We who worked under him were proud of his cold-bloodedness.

—*THE BIG KNOCKOVER* (1924)[*]

Down the years, Hammett must have wondered what might have happened had he gone on chasing crooks for the agency; whether, once he had run out his string as an operative, he could have settled into a desk job bossing younger detectives. His Continental Op certainly speculates about the mental toll of such a life from time to time, still huffing after grifters though he is old enough to leave the field to the kids. The Op fears few things, but one of them is clearly his boss at the Continental's San Francisco branch, known only as the Old Man, a pitiless, white-haired picture of what "fifty years of crook-hunting" can do to a human being. The Old

---

[*] The title was spelled as *The Big Knock-over* in the original 1924 publication, but has been spelled throughout as it was in later reprints.

Man is the Op's cold-blooded future if he stays on, emptied of "everything except brains and a soft-spoken, gently smiling politeness" that is the same no matter how things turn out. Whatever the Op does in the service of his job, he must answer for in his reports to the Old Man, or skirt the truth and risk catching "merry hell." Pontius Pilate, the ops call the Old Man privately, because he smiles sending them out on dicey missions to be "crucified."

The Old Man first turned up in Hammett's story "The Girl with the Silver Eyes" (1924), when the sleeping Op is summoned to the office on a Sunday morning by the "neat," businesslike voice of his boss calling on the phone. Even in stories where he doesn't speak, the Old Man's detectives are often worrying aloud how to explain their code infractions to him. He makes a useful, grounding presence, the figure through which all trails of information converge in the office, and he gives direction to the men's searches in the field: "If the Old Man said something was so, then it probably was, because he was one of these cautious babies who'll look out the window at a cloudburst and say, 'It seems to be raining,' on the off-chance that somebody's pouring water off the roof." The Old Man bears a strong likeness to the best-known Pinkerton detective of all after the founder himself, James McParland,* longtime head of the agency's Western Division, known to his admirers and

---

* He spelled it "McParlan," like generations of his family in Ireland, until sometime in the 1880s, when, perhaps tiring of people hearing the *d* in his name anyway, he decided to legally add it, a small change compared to how so many other immigrants simplified their family names to "Americanize" their identities.

enemies alike simply as the Great Detective. In 1911 the IWW
leader Big Bill Haywood, who had survived a murder charge at
the hands of McParland and Pinkerton's, summed up the
opinion of many in the labor movement:

> When a detective dies, he goes so low that he has to climb a
> ladder to get into Hell—and he is not a welcome guest there.
> When his Satanic Majesty sees him coming, he says to his
> imps, "Go get a big bucket of pitch and a lot of sulphur, give
> them to that fellow and put him outside. Let him start a Hell
> of his own. We don't want him in here, starting trouble."[1]

In the latter years of his fame, with his white hair and
grizzled mustache, his piercing, bespectacled gaze, and his
thick, slouching body that had once been powerful, McParland
looked very much as Hammett's Op describes the Old Man:

> A tall, plump man in his seventies, this boss of mine, with a
> white-mustached, baby-pink, grandfatherly face, mild blue
> eyes behind rimless spectacles, and no more warmth in him
> than a hangman's rope.

During the decades that McParland ran Pinkerton's Western
Division, he made inspection tours of its satellite offices
(Spokane, Seattle, Portland) every few months.[2] As a Pinkerton,
Hammett could not have overlapped with the Great Detective,
as McParland died the same month Hammett was discharged
from the army with TB, in May 1919. But the trail was hardly
cold. Detectives would still be talking about McParland
throughout the agency offices he'd supervised, two of which

(Spokane and Seattle) employed Hammett. McParland's reputation lingered long in San Francisco, too.

Dispatching a crooked superintendent in 1908, McParland
sounds in his report every bit as hard as Hammett's Old Man:

> He said: "What! Am I discharged?" I replied: "Yes, what
> could you expect?" He said: "Won't you allow me to
> resign?," to which I replied: "No, I do not allow a man to
> resign who has admitted himself to be a thief and a forger
> and when conclusive evidence proves him to be a traitor . . .
> A man of your character should be killed and your carcass
> thrown to the dogs and if I killed you, Mr. Cary, in this
> room this minute I would not consider I would have to ask
> the forgiveness of God Almighty for doing so." He immedi-
> ately handed over the keys.[3]

Born in Armagh County, Ireland, in 1843, James McParland
had joined the Agency in Chicago in 1871, after that city's
Great Fire claimed his liquor store. Two years later, he was
working as a conductor on the rear platform of a Chicago
streetcar one day, monitoring employee pilferage for the agency,
when Allan Pinkerton spotted him while considering candi-
dates for the assignment that would earn McParland his newspaper title, the Great Detective: infiltrating an Irish gang of
Pennsylvania miners known secretively as the Sleepers, or
Molly Maguires.

McParland met Pinkerton's criteria for the dangerous
posting: Irish-Catholic, unmarried, gregarious, "hardy, tough,"
and conversant in the history of Northern Ireland's secret
organizations, a subject on which he wrote a seven-page

treatise for his boss to secure the job.* "If this man is mentally correct, and willing," the founder thought, "he is just the instrument fitted for my mining operation."⁴ Adopting an authentically shabby outfit and meticulous cover biography as James McKenna (whose backstory included a murder rap he was fleeing in Buffalo), McParland boarded a train and began wandering the Shenandoah Valley in search of any point of entry to the Mollies. A deadly outgrowth of the labor battles between the mining companies and a weakened union, the Molly Maguires committed acts of terror and murder against company executives as well as fellow miners who displeased them (especially Welshmen). In the late 1860s they killed at least a dozen men per year, a figure that had waned slightly by the time McParland arrived.

As James McKenna, McParland began a terrifying acting job of nearly three years undercover. His approach (later popularized in Allan Pinkerton's *The Mollie Maguires and The Detectives*) has inspired every book or movie since in which a daring agent impersonates a thug to enter a criminal gang—swaggering into their pub headquarters to buy drinks all around, picking a fight with the largest man at hand, charming the gang's leader with a political bar song, and bragging of his out-of-town scrapes with police to gain the thugs' confidence.

---

* The agency was famously stingy with praise for its employees, and McParland's later internal file (from 1880) does not reflect any increased value for his heroism: While his "General deportment and appearance" were considered those of a "genteel Irishman," and he could "readily adapt" to all classes of people, he was rated "not good" as a shadow and his "knowledge of criminals" was considered poor.

The nervous weeks and months spent among his rough cast of new friends caused McParland to drop weight and lose his hair; he finally covered his head with a blond wig. Although he had become a Molly officer, he attempted to quit his Pinkerton's assignment after information he had sent his contact was leaked and led to reprisal killings, including the shooting death of the wife of a Molly. But he was persuaded to stay on undercover, even though this event had cast suspicion among the miners that he was a detective. Eventually McParland had to make his nighttime escape by sleigh ahead of an armed and vengeful gang. Although it put his life further in jeopardy, in 1877 he testified in nine of twenty-three trials; nine Mollies were executed based directly on his testimony, twenty hanged overall.

After the gang had been decimated, McParland tracked down Western train robbers for Pinkerton's before taking charge of the Agency's Denver offices, which he ran almost to the end of his life (although, in 1903 he did write to New York for permission to finally take Sundays off). His fame crested with the 1907 murder case against leaders of the Western Federation of Miners, a conspiracy prosecution McParland seemed to model, rightly or wrongly, on his experience with the Mollies. A secretary at the Denver office later called him, without admiration, "the Dean of Black Sleuthdom."

Hammett's famous Op story "Flypaper" contains a conversation at the Continental office about other celebrated arsenic cases, and the Old Man knowledgeably references various techniques he has seen. In fact, McParland had once solved a nationally known Colorado case—the arsenic poisoning of Mrs. Josephine Barnaby, a widow visiting Denver from Rhode

Island who died in April 1891 after drinking whiskey she had received as a gift in the mail. Unable to lay hands on the likely killer, Mrs. Barnaby's physician and adviser, Thomas Thatcher Graves, who remained safely back east, McParland wrote the culprit a brilliantly fraudulent telegram inviting him to come west to testify and help put away someone else for his own crime. The killer packed at once and was indicted shortly after his arrival in Denver.[5]

Hammett was not the first to use McParland for fiction. The plot of Sir Arthur Conan Doyle's final Sherlock Holmes novel, *The Valley of Fear* (1915), hinges on the career of a former operative named Douglas. It is a hybrid work: a typical Victorian murder mystery set on an English country estate with its own drawbridge gives way to a second tale after the discovery of an ugly American weapon, a sawed-off shotgun traced to Pennsylvania. At one point Holmes hands Douglas a cigar after the former op has given Dr. Watson a manuscript he has written about his undercover days in the Pennsylvania coalfields, a travail that has haunted the rest of his life. "I've heard of you, Mr. Holmes," says ex-detective Douglas. "I never guessed that I should meet you. But before you are through with that [manuscript] you will say that I have brought you something fresh." The honor is clearly a mutual one for the two sleuths, and the scene makes an odd acknowledgment of the "fresh" true story that Watson (Conan Doyle) borrowed to complete the book. (The latter part of the novel, Douglas's savage tale of his undercover life among the American miners, contains neither Holmes nor Watson, who reappear only in the epilogue.)

The inspiration for the novel allegedly struck Conan Doyle when he met William Pinkerton on an Atlantic crossing, the real-life detective entertaining the English author by the fireside with the story of how his agency's super-operative James McParland had brought down the Molly Maguires. Leaning heavily on the earlier account published by Pinkerton's father, Allan, Conan Doyle produced *The Valley of Fear*, an act of appropriation for which William Pinkerton never forgave him. "The entire second part of that book of Doyle's was taken from a book written by my father," he told a reporter. "When I read it I dug up an old copy of my father's book and sent it to Sir Arthur with my compliments. I never received a reply."*

If McParland inspired the characters of both Douglas and the Old Man, then he is the rare real person whose likeness appears in both Hammett and Conan Doyle, a human bridge of sleuthing worlds from the genteel to the hard-boiled.

---

* Whenever William Pinkerton visited London, the tabloids hailed him as the American Sherlock Holmes; while Pinkerton knew the comparison was meant to be honorable, few things displeased him more. Good detecting, he repeated, was based on "common sense," not brilliance.

Chapter IX

BLACKMASKING

*The day is past when I'll fight for the fun of it. But
I've been in too many rumpuses to mind them much.*
—"THE WHOSIS KID" (1925)

O N FEBRUARY 9, 1924, a nurse sent by the U. S. Public
Health Service visited the Crawford Apartments at 620
Eddy Street in San Francisco. Upstairs she found an under-
weight reddish-haired young man waiting for examination. He
complained of weakness and of being easily tired, according to
her report, and looked undernourished and lacking in muscle
development. Sam Hammett admitted he was still not able to
be a detective; he'd given up the part-time work almost exactly
two years before that day's appointment, when another specialist visited him in the Pinkerton offices downtown. But despite
his complaints that were all too familiar, this latest interview
was not all discouraging.[1]

Something distinguished today's physical from so many
others Hammett had endured since the army. For his profession
the ex-detective reported he was working about four hours a

day as a short story writer for magazines, and that his wages depended upon work accepted. Even though his sales at this time can't have been much more than fifty dollars per month,[2] the report lists him as self-employed as a "story-writer." While admitting he was too sick for conventional work, Hammett was proud enough of his recent success to boast of it to a government nurse, even if it threatened the calculation of the pension that fed his family.

As sick and poor as he was, Hammett had a right to brag about his growing career writing for magazines. Despite his health, in 1923 he had published sixteen stories and essays in six separate magazines. Some of it was subpar work, highlighting an understandable hunger for steady sales, but there were also longer stories showing the writer he could become, with situations and themes he would revisit in his novels.

Following his secretarial course all the way through would have trained him to be a stenographer. He had completed enough training to learn what he needed of touch typing, and since his hospitalization the previous October, his disability had been restored to 50 percent. If he could keep at it, he now had skills for working faster and longer in what he hoped was his new profession.

In July 1923 *The New Pearson's* published a rare autobiographical sketch of his called "Holiday," a short third-person story about a day in the life of a young lunger named Paul Hetherwick, who leaves his San Diego hospital with a day pass and visits Tijuana, where he gambles on horses, drinks with a veteran "subharlot" at one bar, and then with a younger redheaded woman whose attractiveness unnerves him in the tumbledown setting. At the end of the night, he heads home to the hospital broke but well-oiled, pleased to be riding up top on the night coach. This unaffected little story remains the most successful writing Hammett published that was drawn directly from his own life: on his day away from the doctors, Paul smokes cigars, drinks himself nearly insensible, and rides home coughing into the chilly fog, defying his condition in a way that Hammett thought the disease respected. The following year, he would send his Continental Op to revisit the seedy strip of Tijuana saloons and their rugged hostesses in "The Golden Horseshoe."

While a bit clunkier, "Laughing Masks" (which ran in *Action Stories*, November 1923) was his longest (thirteen thousand words) and most ambitious story yet, starring not his Op but a low-level gambler whose investigation of a startling scream draws him into trouble. The story incorporated San Francisco settings of the day with a hint of the writer's own experiences, such as being hit over the head: "A white flame seared his eyeballs; the ground went soft and billowy under his feet, as if it were part of the fog . . . Phil sat up on the wet paving and felt his head. His fingers found a sore, swelling area running from above the left ear nearly to the crown."[3]

Evolving from detective to writer, or from Sam to Dash, Hammett had still signed letters to Jose as "Sam" or "S.D.H." in the early twenties, but became "Dashiell Hammett" to his editors, a second self gradually eclipsing his legal identity. By 1924, the year he turned thirty, he was becoming the emerging voice of *The Black Mask*, which increasingly favored a violent realism over classic detection and was the most significant of the tier of pulp crime magazines Hammett was now mining.

The Black Mask's new editor, Phil Cody, hailed Hammett as "one of our most popular authors."

His stories were getting longer and better. "The Tenth Clew," his first real jewel of a story, came out in *The Black Mask* in January 1924, earning him his first cover the month before his boastful visit with the government nurse. "The Tenth Clew" presents an unusual challenge for the Op in that he has a misleading surplus of evidence. (As Hammett points out in "From the Memoirs of a Private Detective," the fictional detective typically faces "a paucity of clues," while a real sleuth has "altogether too many" to sort through.) Only by throwing away much of his hard-earned knowledge of the case can the Op get his man, and even so he ends up slugged and thrown overboard from a ferry, which leads to Hammett's beautiful evocation of coming awake in the dark, foggy bay:

> A light glimmered mistily off to my left, and then vanished. From out of the misty blanket, from every direction, in a dozen different keys, from near and far, fog horns sounded. I stopped swimming and floated on my back, trying to determine my whereabouts.

"Zigzags of Treachery" (also from early 1924) is almost too trickily plotted for Hammett's new kind of realistic action-detective story—featuring an imposter with two wives, a blackmailer, an elaborately faked copy of a newspaper, a shooting death in a study, and a suppressed suicide note—but the Op's energetic shadowing pulls you along on his gumshoe rounds while his wisecracking nicely masks the fancier sleuthing, "She didn't buy anything, but she did a lot of thorough looking, with me muddling along behind her, trying to act like a little fat guy on an errand for his wife."

As he typed them in his kitchen, Hammett's Op stories seemed to improve almost with each effort, except for two that were publicly rejected that summer by *The Black Mask*'s editors, who were raising their magazine's standards and focusing its mission more on a certain kind of action-driven story, a standard inspired by Hammett's own work. A column for the August 1924 issue, Our Own Short Story Course, was strangely devoted to their decision to slap the hand of their rising star, followed by the writer's even stranger note of contrition: "The trouble is this sleuth of mine has degenerated into a meal-ticket," Hammett wrote. "I liked him at first and used to enjoy putting him through his tricks; but recently I've fallen into the habit of bringing him out and running him around whenever the landlord, or the butcher, or the grocer shows signs of nervousness."[4]

Thanking his editors for "jolting me into wakefulness," Hammett resolved, "There's no telling how much good this will do me" and vowed to put the offending stories into a deep drawer. Presumably, it was Hammett's supplicating answer that inspired the magazine to present the correspondence as a teaching course to warn off lazier submissions. But the low rate *Black Mask*'s editors were still paying their rising star should have been insult enough, without Hammett's having to apologize for trying to make a living. Needing money more than he needed to feel pure, Hammett sold them a revision of one of the previously rejected tales, "Women, Politics & Murder," for that fall, although it remained a subpar story. The other, an Op story retitled "Who Killed Bob Teal?" ran in the November

True Detective Stories with the byline "Dashiell Hammett of the Continental Detective Agency." The Hammett of three years later would not have wasted his time renegotiating a story sale at pennies per word. As he wrote Alfred A. Knopf's editors in 1930, irked by someone's red markings, "I am returning your invoice for excess corrections on *The Glass Key* . . . [Y]ou'll see you're very lucky I haven't billed you for the trouble I was put to unediting it."

Sometime in late 1924 or early 1925, Hammett, whose stoicism about his disease seemingly had no limit, became convinced by doctors that his TB had blown up enough that he had to live apart from his family rather than risk passing it on to his young daughter. He secured a larger apartment downstairs at Eddy Street and kept writing. For a time they may have kept both apartments, before reuniting downstairs, where he graduated from working at the kitchen table to his own writing desk.*

In late 1924, he published "Ruffian's Wife," about a young woman who fills her days cheerfully cleaning her apartment

---

* Since the emergence of photos of Jose and her girls in Anaconda from the fall of 1926, it is clear they went there then. But this earlier separation is hardly settled: Some accounts have them escaping to Anaconda in 1924–25, while others send them off to a little house in Fairfax, California, in 1924. Mary Jane Hammett says 1925 in the Fechheimer interview, but she also says her new sister, Jo, was there, which means it was after the latter's birth in May 1926. Jo herself mentions the Fairfax house as the place the three went *after* their six-month Anaconda trip in 1926, and that she learned to walk there. I see no reason to believe they didn't just move downstairs to a larger place at Eddy Street, perhaps briefly separating within the same building, during the scare of 1924–25.

awaiting the return of her brutal slob of a husband on the ferry. Like his taut Western story "The Man Who Killed Dan Odams" and the surprise tale "The Second Story Angel," in which a lady burglar fools a group of crime writers, Hammett showed he could bring off a story with a female character who was not just a femme fatale and was unlike the dames and baby dolls presented by his colleagues then in the pulps. "Ruffian's Wife" also shows his early fondness for cinematic nighttime gunfights, what he called "shots in the dark."

He called the writing he was doing "Blackmasking," and sometimes recorded two thousand words in a day. Closing out the year, in December 1924 he published "Nightmare Town" in *Argosy All-Story*. It was a non-Op adventure, but one that would lay out the basic theme of his first novel, *Red Harvest*, about a town so wholly decayed with corruption, down to its last seemingly innocent old man, that it has to be destroyed to be saved. Such towns were not hard to imagine in the gangster-ridden age Prohibition had made possible. The growing sense of institutional corruption and lawlessness around the country was also shaping the public's appetite for stories about lone private detectives who kept their own personal code.

From March to December of 1925, he published five superb stories at the more ambitious length that *The Black Mask*'s editors called "novelettes," starting with a misadventure among thieves called "The Whosis Kid" (a seductive criminal betrays her male accomplices while trying to seduce the law in a preview of *The Maltese Falcon*); followed by "The Scorched Face," in which the Op's investigation involves missing rebellious girls, an orgiastic cult, blackmail, and a rash of suicides— about as much as a writer could get away with presenting in the

1920s. "Corkscrew" allowed Hammett to take the Op out of his element and into the shimmery desert of an Arizona range war, where he plays the rival cowboys and desperadoes against one another, but gains the trust of some gunslingers by getting himself repeatedly thrown from the horse they have prankishly recommended.

Hammett ended the year with his little detective in a running gun battle after the looting of a fictional island off the Northern California coast, "The Gutting of Couffignal." But his first small masterpiece was one he set in a place that to most readers was still at least half-myth, Chinatown.

He had wandered all over San Francisco in his fiction before writing his most sophisticated story yet, the anachronistically titled "Dead Yellow Women." It added Chinatown to his territory, edging his crime plot with deadpan satire of the then popular novels about Dr. Fu Manchu, while also spoofing the exoticism of Caucasian writers who used Chinatown as a setting for white slaver stories of beautiful tourists grabbed from opium dens.

In "Dead Yellow Women" a multiple murder case is brought to the agency by a wealthy young woman named Lillian Sheen, whose late father brought her from Manchuria as a girl. The investigation of the murders leads the Op to Chinatown, "a strip two blocks wide by six long," for an audience with Chang Li Ching, the patriarch of the Chinese underworld. The Op turns off Grant Avenue, with its "gaudy shops and flashy chop suey houses," at Clay Street and into a short dead-end block of unmarked gambling houses called Spofford Alley. Which door the Op takes next is where the story leaves the known map. Only on paper is this still the Op's town. He leaves the San

Francisco he knows through a door "the color of dried blood,"*
following a network of dark passageways.

Pushing through the comically long warren, the Op is nearly
shot by his own hop head contact, Dummy Uhl, who is hiding
in the dark. At last the Op emerges into a curtained room
where he meets his match in Chang Li Ching, his face "round
and plump and shrewd, with a straggle of thin, white whiskers."
Chang speaks in "a burlesque . . . of the well-known Chinese
politeness," spoof-honoring his visitor as the "Grandduke
of Manhunters," "Disperser of Marauders," and "Master of
Mysteries." The Op jests back at this old man, whose harsh
justice in the case he needs. Later, after Chang discovers that
the Op has tricked him into killing, he sends a note to the
"Emperor of Untanglers." The story ends with the Op's chilled
aside, "I don't mind admitting that I've stopped eating in
Chinese restaurants, and that if I never have to visit Chinatown
again it'll be soon enough."

With a plot grounded in Prohibition smuggling and
Manchurian politics, "Dead Yellow Women" ran in the
November 1925 issue of *The Black Mask*. It hides Hammett's
library research more smoothly than earlier efforts, and showed
a new level of accomplishment, being satirical while still deliv-
ering a good, tense crime story, well above what else was being
published in *The Black Mask* at the time, a balance Hammett

---

* Visiting Spofford Alley now, with its Yin-Yin Music Association sign
tucked away among massage and reflexology places, it is hard to guess which
red door Hammett intended. But the myths were so thick about Chinatown
that it might as well have been any of them.

would later forget how to achieve. It remains the favorite Op story of his daughter Jo.

He was now gaining a readership, but despite the popularity of his Op, his writing still did not command a price his family could live on. His influence on *The Black Mask* was undeniable by 1925–26, where authentic new writers were appearing whose menacing work sprang at least allegedly from street experience—storytellers who were motorcycle patrolmen by day or who had paid their realist dues as police reporters. Instead of the standard drawing-room detective story, where the plot's neat payoff justified everything, recalled Raymond Chandler, who followed Hammett into the pulps, in the new "*Black Mask* type of story . . . the scene outranked the plot, in the sense that a good plot was one which made good scenes. The ideal mystery was one you would read if the end was missing."[5]

In the fall of 1925, Jose became pregnant with their second child. Hammett began to interest himself in advertising writing, another creative form that seemed to pay much better. He studied advertising theory at the public library as much as he could, and in December he became a regular reviewer for *Western Advertising* magazine.

Despite the emergence of this hard-boiled school in which he was prominent, Hammett couldn't get a raise. Early in 1926 he had a falling out with *Black Mask*'s editor, Phil Cody, over money. Hammett's fellow contributor Erle Stanley Gardner (who later created Perry Mason) offered that Cody dock Gardner a penny per word off his own rate and add it to Hammett's if it meant Hammett's work could stay in the magazine. The strange but heartfelt offer was refused by the publisher, and Hammett left *Black Mask*. Circulation soon fell to sixty-six thousand, and Cody quit as editor.[6]

Sometime during the winter through the spring of 1925 to 1926, a desperate Hammett took out a classified ad asking for any available work, and boasting ". . . and I can write." This may have brought him to the attention of Albert Samuels Jewelers, but he was more likely already freelancing there when he heard about a full-time position as advertising manager.

Chapter X

THE PRICE OF PEGGY O'TOOLE

"Hello, Bernie. This is Ned. What's the price on
Peggy O'Toole?"

—THE GLASS KEY (1931)

G OING TO AND FROM the Pinkerton offices in the Flood
Building when he was still an operative, Hammett had
certainly noticed Albert Samuels Jewelers, "The House of
Lucky Wedding Rings," nearby on Market Street, with its
familiar sidewalk clock. Inside each of the company's wedding
bands was the trademark inscription A.S. LUCKY, since they
claimed to ensure a durable marriage, and Samuels held an
annual party for as many of the couples as he could accommodate who had sealed their vows with his rings.

Samuels liked his employees almost as much as his customers, and his shop and upstairs offices had a family atmosphere.
A newspaper picture from December 1922 shows Samuels
Jewelers' happy staff, all eighty of them from his combined
stores, arranged along covered banquet tables at the company's
yearly dinner dance in the Hotel Whitcomb. The rows of

dark-suited men and floral-dressed women intersect the square pillars of the hotel dining room; twenty-three of them were native Californians, Samuels reported, with the remainder including enough "representatives of many foreign countries— that a customer who couldn't talk English might summon some member of our force and have the subject expounded to him fluently in his own tongue . . ."[1] After his lonely months struggling at home, Hammett must have been thrilled, when he made his skinny-dapper entrance, to be part of such a cosmopolitan workplace.

Samuels's firm was well known for its wide use of newspaper ads, some of them written by Albert himself, but others, before Hammett joined the company, created by a young man named Jay H. Haight, who had come up with the idea of sponsoring free classifieds to reunite people with their lost jewelry, regardless of its origin. "We hope to profit by the gratitude and the good will of those we assist," Haight told a reporter. "Also we may occasionally pick up a job of repairing."[2] These seemingly selfless classifieds were a success and a steady source of warm anecdotes of people's reunions with their missing brooches, bar pins, or gold tortoiseshell glasses. Samuels's ads in general were direct and often told an emotional story, a form Hammett could easily get the knack of.

Al Samuels would later remember being introduced to Hammett by a mutual friend as late as 1926, the year the writer began full time. But, being an observant type who liked nice things, Hammett would have been aware of the diamond shop much earlier as a Pinkerton, and may have begun freelancing for Samuels at the end of 1925, when he had begun reviewing books on advertising. Unlike some other novelists of his time who saw advertising as a means to keep them in whiskey and typewriter ribbon, Hammett took an interest in the new writing challenges of this format, something that could be done well or badly and that paid much better than the freelance story market at the time. As he had said rather stiffly in a recent book review, "The eternal problem of the creative worker in whatever field is to bring his whole mind, his every faculty, to bear on the task under his hand." Hammett had never learned to look down on what he was doing.

Since most newspaper copy for the store was signed by Samuels himself, it is difficult to gauge exactly where Hammett broke in, but it seems unlikely he would have been hired on directly, a man who had not worked full time since 1918, without some kind of part-time trial. In the end, Samuels would become one of Hammett's most unshakeable friends, a kind of literary benefactor to whom he dedicated his second novel, *The Dain Curse*, which opens with a search for eight stolen diamonds.

On the many postcards he drew for his friends and children, Hammett showed a spare, Thurber-like line as an amateur cartoonist. Soon he was overseeing the clean look of the firm's print ads as well as their texts in which crises were resolved for young men who had foolishly bought "size" over "quality" and whose lifeless engagement stones were replaced with brilliant blue-white diamonds in time to save the marriage. "Nothing you can wear adds more to your appearance than good jewelry," began one Samuels ad of her husband's, lovingly saved by Mrs. Hammett. "Tastefully selected, properly worn, it will do for your dress what eyes do for your face—make it live with points of fire and color."[3]

Once on staff as advertising manager, Hammett made $350 per month, doubling his income just as he had become a father again, with the arrival of Josephine Rebecca Hammett (later called Jo) on May 24, 1926. He now worked a six-day week alongside sophisticated people who went drinking after work. Jose Hammett later blamed her husband's increased drinking and carousing on the stint at the Samuels office. But the predilection was already in him; he just hadn't the money or stable health for stepping out, and never knew how long the TB would lie quiet.

In his new surroundings, he focused particularly on Peggy O'Toole, a young art assistant with whom he chose to have an affair. "She was one of the rare red-haired women whose skins are without blemish," he wrote in a story he sent her; "she was marble, to the eye." O'Toole, he later told their mutual boss, inspired Hammett to create Brigid O'Shaughnessy, whose dark red hair curling beneath her blue hat is among the first things Sam Spade catalogues as she crosses the office threshold into his life in *The Maltese Falcon*. As Hammett described the flesh-and-blood Peggy O'Toole in 1926:

> One otherwise dreary afternoon she lay with her bright red head on my knees while I read Don Marquis' *Sonnets to a Red Haired Lady* to her. When I had finished she made a little purring noise and stared dreamily distant-eyed past me, "Tell me about this Don Marquis," she said. "Do you know him?"[4]

O'Toole, who had also been told she inspired *Red Harvest*'s Dinah Brand, eventually married someone else from the

Samuels office, a man who did not like to be reminded even decades later of her connection to literature. Hammett was still thinking of her when he wrote *The Glass Key* in 1930, in which Ned Beaumont spends the early part of the book chasing his winnings on a horse named Peggy O'Toole, leading to another gambler's greeting, "Heard you had Peggy O'Toole today."[5]

One day in the mid-1970s, Peggy found herself facing another San Francisco detective, who had followed Hammett's winding old trail to her doorstep. During this same time, David Fechheimer had turned up Hammett's former Pinkerton partner Phil Haultain and a contemporary from the Agency, Jack Kaplan; he found Mrs. Josephine Hammett, still living in Los Angeles with the couple's older daughter, Mary; and he made a discovery he couldn't put in print with the others.

Standing out front all these years later, Peggy explained to Fechheimer that she couldn't let him into her house because her husband didn't like her talking about her relationship with Hammett, whose letters she had nevertheless kept, whether as his old girlfriend or muse; in fact, she warned the young detective, her husband was "still pissed about it."[*]

★   ★   ★

---

[*] Author's correspondence with Fechheimer. The interview with Peggy O'Toole did not make its way into the all-Hammett issue of *City of San Francisco* Magazine (Nov. 4, 1975), which included the full sixty-five-page draft of Hammett's abandoned original *Thin Man* novel, set in San Francisco. The *City* issue added to the drumbeat for a planned film based on the Joe Gores novel, *Hammett*, produced by Francis Ford Coppola, the publisher of *City*. The issue, without which no Hammett biography of the past forty years would be possible, now sells for $150 online.

HOWEVER ABLE HE was at his job, during his first months working for Samuels, Hammett was pushing himself too hard, keeping bad hours, and drinking far too much, often during the day. It is a testament to Albert Samuels's fondness for Hammett that he didn't fire him for his disruptive drinking, as he would have another employee. Perhaps he had a different standard for men who were writers. But the question became moot when, on the afternoon of July 20, 1926, his advertising manager collapsed in the office and was found unconscious and lying in what Samuels called a pool of blood from his hemorrhaging lungs. If found much later, Hammett might have choked to death on his own blood. In addition to the TB, he was discovered to also have hepatitis. He had lasted five hard-driving months working full time when he returned home, as sick as he had ever been, to the bed from which he had risen before.

As his convalescence dragged into September, Samuels, ever the gentleman employer, gave Hammett a notarized letter to provide to the Veterans' Bureau in hopes of starting up his relief again:

Gentlemen,

This is to certify that Samuel Dashiell Hammett resigned his position as advertising manager of the Albert S. Samuels on July 20, 1926, because ill health had made it impossible for him to perform his duties.

Very truly yours,

Albert S. Samuels

Doctors insisted that a family with a new baby needed to be physically separated from such an active TB case. This time,

Jose took the girls with her all the way home by train to Anaconda, for a separation that would last six months. Hammett's disability was once again listed as total.

During his sickest times at Eddy Street, Hammett set up a network of chairs for making his way across the living room to the kitchen and bath or to occasionally spit blood. The story of the chairs later became a kind of origins tale or symbol of his remarkable tenacity—the tough guy leaving his bed of pain to keep working. ("When he wrote *Red Harvest*, friends say," the *Los Angeles Times* repeated in 1934, "he was so ill, he had to line up the furniture between chair and typewriter to lean on as he dragged himself back and forth.") But his separation from his family did not at first force him to develop his fiction art; he was once again desperate for money.

Hammett soon tried to reestablish himself full time as an ad man, battling at the office with a new rival named Chipman, who, said Hammett, would "slit my throat" if given the chance. Samuels was understandably cautious about giving Hammett the entire office load he had carried before his collapse. Though often boastful after his office debates about advertising, in October, Hammett wrote his wife in Montana a surprisingly fragile letter about his situation with Samuels: "I'd like to know whether anything is going to come of the advertising racket or not. What he's [Samuels] afraid of is that I'll die on his hands. I'm not altogether sure I want the blooming thing."[6] Imagining the work and added bickering of coming back and fighting for his old position, he explained, "I don't know whether that will sit well on my lungs or not."

Nevertheless, he kept building his industry reputation by writing essays such as "Advertising IS Literature," which ran in the October 1926 *Western Advertising*. "Whether he likes it not," Hammett wrote from experience, "every man who works with words for effects is a literary worker." The worker's only "liberty" was "in deciding how adept he shall be."

As he was building his career back up with Samuels, a man named Joseph Shaw took the helm of *The Black Mask*. He quickly dropped "The" from its title and began assigning for the fall of 1926. Starting out as a newspaperman, Shaw had been known as "Cap" to his friends since the Great War, in which he attained captain's rank as a bayonet instructor. He had also been a national champion in sabers. A man with little experience editing magazines, he nevertheless had a clear idea for the intriguing enterprise he had been handed.

One of the most important goals Shaw set for himself was to bring Dashiell Hammett and his popular Op back into the fold. Neither had appeared in *Black Mask* since March 1926. Shaw wrote Hammett a letter in which he pledged him more money and proposed longer works, to be serialized by *Black Mask*, stretching beyond the constraints of the magazine story form. Hammett was delighted; it was, he said, just what he had had in mind himself, and he seemed especially pleased that Shaw was paying him the three hundred dollars Hammett felt his predecessor Phil Cody still owed him. Hammett usually called it "applesauce" when people praised him while wanting something, but he reported it proudly to his wife.

That fall of 1926, a nurse named Esther Haley, who special-ized in TB cases, found Hammett living alone briefly at 20 Monroe Place; on a follow-up in November, she saw him at 1309 Hyde Street, where the whole family was reunited in an arrangement that nevertheless passed Nurse Haley's inspection for hygiene: the patient had a room to himself away from the children. She noted that his weight was up ten pounds and, while he still had night sweats, he said he was doing some writing for magazines. When Haley saw him next, in March 1927, Hammett was alone in a studio at 891 Post Street, still resting, he told her, but also doing advertising work from home. The wife and children, Haley recorded, lived in an apartment on Sacramento, near Hyde. By April's exam, he explained he was a little worse, although with no blood spitting, and that his rotten teeth bothered him tremendously.[7]

During this time, he had nevertheless written something extraordinary for Cap Shaw, a novella called *The Big Knockover*. He was also now reviewing mysteries for the *Saturday Review of Literature*, a platform he relished, raising himself and his realist school of detective fiction even as he pointed out the weak stew served by others. His focus had switched back almost entirely to writing. In the January 1927 *Black Mask*, Shaw announced Hammett's coming return in the next issue: "Dashiell Hammett has called back the Continental detective from his long retirement and is setting him to work anew."

When it began running in excerpts in February 1927, *The Big Knockover* featured a brazen, over-the-top double holdup of San Francisco banks, one of which may have been modeled on the Old Mint building. You can feel Hammett stretching out at last, achieving the full, striding voice of his longer works. "I found Paddy the Mex in Jean Larrouy's dive," it begins,

Paddy—an amiable con man who looked like the King of Spain—showed me his big white teeth in a smile, pushed a chair out for me with one foot, and told the girl who shared his table:

"Nellie, meet the biggest-hearted dick in San Francisco. This little fat guy will do anything for anybody, if only he can send 'em over for life in the end."

The Big Knockover has many elements: spare, slangy prose; the Op's serving as guide to scruffy locales up and down San Francisco; and poetic lists of criminal names, proof of Hammett's strong grounding in Pinkerton studies. It also features a criminal operation seemingly far larger than the Op or the police force of his wide-open town can handle.

The Op is skeptical when he first hears of the audacious bank "caper" from a stuttering newsie, but his source is gunned down moments later by a young Armenian boy who saunters off "hands in pockets, softly whistling *Broken-Hearted Sue.*" Intrigued by a traffic jam he sees on Market Street the next day, the Op walks over toward the Financial District and the Seaman's Bank. As he gets closer, he hears "roaring, rattling, explosive noises" and sees a man trying to set his dislocated jaw back in place. Finally, he reaches the block between Bush and Pine Streets, where "Hell was on a holiday." Where the Seaman's National and Golden Gate Trust Company buildings face each other, a double looting is going on, involving a robbery gang of perhaps a hundred and fifty crooks. "For the next six hours," says the Op, "I was busier than a flea on a fat woman."

Inspiring his own epic heist, Hammett had certainly read a national news story about a bold posse of gunmen making a raid on the Denver Federal Reserve Bank in December 1922.

Firing their way in during business hours, they got away with two hundred thousand dollars, the record daylight take at the time, shooting up the streetscape as they sped off under fire from overwhelmed upstairs guards, one of whom died of his wounds. As he fired from the running board of the getaway car, one of the robbers was hit but was pulled inside it as the gang sped off.[8]

What follows in *The Big Knockover* is a detecting adventure as it had never been done. In a room on Fillmore Street, the Op catalogues the notable dead crooks he recognizes on the floor, from the Dis-and-Dat Kid, "who had crushed out of Leavenworth only two months before"; to Snohomish Whitey, "supposed to have died a hero in France in 1919"; to "L.A. Slim, from Denver, sockless and underwearless as usual, with a thousand dollar bill sewed in each shoulder of his coat"; to Bull McGonickle, "still pale from fifteen years in Joliet"; to Toby the Lugs, "Bull's running mate, who used to brag about picking President Wilson's pocket in a Washington vaudeville theater"; to Paddy the Mex. The Agency's founder, Allan Pinkerton, might have appreciated the low-life scholarship of such a list.

If you consider *The Big Knockover* together with its follow-up, "$106, 000 Blood Money," which began running in May, the two parts make up Hammett's first novel. However, their author didn't see them that way and would not have his linked novellas published together.

By the baby's first birthday that May, Jose and the girls had moved across the bay to a little house in Fairfax, California, where Hammett would visit them by ferry once or twice each week, and where baby Jo eventually learned to walk. By the end of 1927, doctors would tell him his TB was gone, but

Hammett stayed on at 891 Post Street, in a studio he would later come to share with Sam Spade.

For his first published novel, he chose to take his Op on his bloodiest mission yet, away from the bay and up north into the mountains and the labor wars in Montana. With pressure from his *Black Mask* editors for ever more action, he chose a place he knew whose starkness and violence needed little exaggeration.

Chapter XI

THE BIG SHIP

*"This damned burg's getting me. If I don't get away
soon I'll be going blood-simple like the natives."*
—THE CONTINENTAL OP IN *RED HARVEST*

YOU SEE THE cindery hillside with a high funnel sticking out of it, a masonry smokestack almost six hundred
feet tall, for a long time on the dusty approach to the town.
And as you enter the small, flat grid of streets the stack hovers
darkly over your shoulder on its slag-covered mound, while
here and there, among the lines of houses and brick storefronts,
appear Deco–style holdovers such as the Washoe theater or
Club Moderne.

Anaconda was founded in 1883 by a copper magnate named
Marcus Daly, who had bought the nearby Anaconda mine and
hoped to make his company town the capital of Montana. In
Hammett's novel *Red Harvest*, the Continental Op arrives in
a grim 1920s mining town called Personville ("Poisonville"
to locals) that shares some details with Anaconda. Marcus
Daly's story could be an inspiration for Personville's old

mining "czar" Elihu Willsson, who "owned Personville, heart, soul, skin and guts" for forty years until 1921, when he paid an army of goons to help him break the miners' union: "When the last skull had been cracked, the last rib kicked in, organized labor in Personville was a used firecracker"— but at a price. Like other nightmare towns Hammett wrote about, Personville had gone to the thugs. A city owned and run by Elihu Willsson had degenerated into a criminal free-for-all.

Personville conflates Anaconda with nearby Butte and the smaller mining village whose name it echoes, Walkerville. But it actually borrows more from Butte:

> The city wasn't pretty. Most of its builders had gone in for gaudiness. Since then the smelters whose brick stacks stuck up tall against a gloomy mountain to the south had yellow-smoked everything into uniform dinginess. The result was an ugly city of forty thousand people, set in an ugly notch between two ugly mountains that had been all dirtied up by mining.[1]

The story opens with the Op having a drink in a real Butte location, the Big Ship, a miner's nickname for Butte's biggest boardinghouse, the Florence Hotel. The real Butte was certainly set "in a notch between two mountains," a hillside town running up to the Mountain Meadow cemetery where the body of Frank Little was carried by grieving miners in 1917.

Like Butte at this time, Personville had a "Broadway line," which the Op rides to visit Elihu Willsson, whose home corresponds on the map to where the surviving home of another copper king, William A. Clark, sits in Butte.²*

The Op is called to town by Elihu Willsson's son, Donald, who, as the editor of one of his father's newspapers, has been naïvely running a reformist campaign to clean up Personville. Donald Willsson is quickly killed before the two men can meet, and not wanting to waste the trip from San Francisco, the Op gets himself hired by old Elihu himself to restore the town he once ran.

Elihu's check for ten thousand dollars to the Continental Detective Agency unleashes the bloodletting to come as the Op sets to work pitting the gang members against one another to empty Personville "of its crooks and grafters." At one point a battered black touring car whips past him "crammed to the curtains with men," and the Op grins with pride: "Poisonville was beginning to boil out under the lid." The Op has a dark gift for sowing violence, cracking open the weak confederacies of criminals, and tying up loose ends outside the courts. This is put on spectacular display in Personville, where he quickly sizes up police chief Noonan as helpless and genially corrupt. Hammett knew that the real Butte bloomed with such evil characters—soiled lawmen such as the former chief detective Ed Morrisey, who was not unlike the sorry ex-detective Bob MacSwain in *Red Harvest*. Fired as a violent drunkard and

---

* Clark, who beat Marcus Daly in the dirty campaign over a state capital, owned the Butte streetcar system that brought visitors to his thirty-four-room Victorian mansion. For an entertaining account of the battles between the magnates, see C. B. Glasscock, *The War of The Copper Kings* (New York: Grosset and Dunlap, 1935).

suspected (but never charged) in the death of his wife, Morrissey also hired himself out as a gunman and was discussed for decades as a suspect in the Frank Little killing. (A citizen definitely worthy of Poisonville, Morrissey was found beaten to death in 1922.)[3]

At the center of the storm he has caused, the Op finds a lucky ally in Dinah Brand, a "deluxe hustler" and gossipy moll who greets him with a "soft, lazy" voice. She has "the face of a girl of twenty-five already showing signs of wear," her part is crooked, her rouge uneven, her dress is "a particularly unbecoming wine color," and one stocking has a run, but, the Op deadpans, "This was the Dinah Brand who took her pick of Poisonville's men, I had been told." He warms to her, too, as she matches him drink for drink while dangling criminal gossip for sale: "I'm a girl who likes to pick up a little jack when she can." She sketches for him the town's outlaw cast of bootleggers, grifters, and crooked cops, but wants payment: "You can think it's not going to cost you anything, but I'll get mine before we're through," she says. Recognizing the Op's mission, she offers, "If stirring things up is your system, I've got a swell spoon for you."[4]

Dinah Brand is probably the most lifelike female character Hammett ever created, and as with a number of his fictional people, she was probably modeled in part on some vivid acquaintance; she resembles a type of woman he favored in his dalliances, "rumpled, frowsy, edging into blowsy," as Jo Hammett describes her in *A Daughter Remembers*, "and perfectly comfortable with herself and with men—the kind of woman, I noticed over the years, that my father was attracted to."[5] It is hard to know if, while writing his Poisonville novel, Hammett was already spending time with Nell Martin, the spirited woman who would later accompany him to New York. "I used to think I knew men," Dinah complains at one point, "but, by God! I don't. They're lunatics, all of them."*

Not only does the Op get a disturbing taste for death in Personville, but he befriends this woman who seems to have already fleeced many of the town's men, except for the passive lunger she keeps around to abuse, Dan Rolff. When the Op uncharacteristically confesses to Dinah that he fears he is "going blood-simple like the natives," she comforts him with laudanum, and he has two gumshoeing hallucinations, as dogged as they are poetic. In one, he trails after a woman whose face is hidden by a veil, following her voice through "half the streets in the United States"; in the second dream, he chases around a strange city "a small brown man who wore an immense sombrero":

> Keeping one hand on the open knife in my pocket, I ran toward the little brown man, running on the heads and shoulders of the people in the plaza. The heads and shoulders were of unequal heights and unevenly spaced. I slipped and floundered over them.[6]

The Op wakes to a worse nightmare: he is gripping a fatal ice pick. Thinking he was solving one crime, he also must clear

---

* In later years, as he continued to be compared to Ernest Hemingway—who also wrote sparely about tough guys but was never labeled a genre writer—Hammett would insist to friends that "Ernest" did not create convincing female characters—none as lifelike as Dinah Brand, anyway.

himself of Dinah's murder. He has gone "native" to the point that even one of his steadiest fellow operatives, the terse Canadian Dick Foley, becomes unsure of his innocence; enough so that the Op sends him back to San Francisco. The book ends with the Op fretting over the language of his agency reports to the Old Man but still catching "merry hell" for his tactics.

One mystery at the center of this book is how Hammett wrote something so convincingly realistic. The traditional account suggests that his first novel grew out of the nightmarish things he saw during his brief time spent in Butte as a Pinkerton, when dozens of agents roamed undercover on behalf of the mining companies. It seems quite a leap of faith to accept Hammett's story about being in Butte in 1917, when he was a relatively new operative in Baltimore, and being offered a bribe to kill Frank Little. But it is not impossible he was there in 1920, the year of a second round of strikes, riots, shootings, and federal troops, when he worked out of the Spokane office. This hews more closely to how the Pinkerton Agency functioned, assigning from the Denver office and drawing operatives primarily from other northwest branches. More easily dispatched from Spokane than from Baltimore, Hammett may have done some service working undercover, if he was healthy enough, between his move west to Spokane in May 1920 and his collapse that November, after which he went off to the Cushman hospital to meet the young nurse who became his wife.

Like so much with Hammett in the early twenties, even if on paper he should have been immobilized, it does not mean he obeyed. If he came to Butte that spring, he would have arrived just weeks after the Anaconda Road Massacre of April 21, 1920, an event in which sixteen striking miners were shot from behind during a protest outside the Neversweat Mine, and another, Tom Manning, died later from his wounds. Troops returned to Butte, but calm had not been entirely restored when Hammett would have walked its streets.

There is another, more literary reason to believe he was there in 1920: he describes the town too well not to have seen it. Another possibility, that he visited his wife and daughters there in 1926, when his TB became contagious and when Jose brought the girls home to Anaconda, is not likely and is not how the family remembered it: he was far too sick in 1926 for such a long train trip. Being such a gifted observer, Hammett only needed to visit Butte for a week or so to be able to describe things he saw and, especially, heard in billiard halls, hotel lobbies, and the precinct house; or at the fights; or in the room of an appealingly disheveled young woman. He also had another source for background, though she rarely gets credit.

His authenticity, the "skin of realism" of his writing, springs from Hammett's own detecting experiences. However, his wife, Jose, had grown up in the dingy model town for Poisonville, and would have known her way around it in all its ugliness. She knew the violent history from her vantage point as the adopted daughter of "Captain" William Kelly, an executive at the Anaconda Copper Mining Company. Even if she didn't present what she remembered in the style Hammett preferred, her memories would have made excellent atmosphere for a novelist to tease out and rearrange however he liked.

According to his granddaughter Julie Rivett, Hammett's daughter Jo remembered that he "got irritated with her mother when she talked about the strikes in Anaconda. Grandma, I'm told, described in positive terms how the strikebreakers were given special privileges—extra food, chocolates, and such. To her, it seemed a wonder."[7] Hammett, who had known strikebreaking more intimately, had not experienced it as wondrous or privileged work but as an ugly and dangerous assignment. Still, despite the gulf in their perspectives, it is hard to dispute he would have gleaned meaningful background from Jose when creating the world of Personville.

"The Cleansing of Poisonville" began appearing serially in *Black Mask* in November 1927. The magazine's editors hailed the debut of "the first, complete, episode in a series dealing with a city whose administrators have gone mad with power and lust of wealth. It is also, to our minds, the ideal detective story—the new type of detective fiction which *Black Mask* is seeking to develop . . . Poisonville is written by a master of his craft."

For all that, Hammett still had to send off his "Poisonville" novel unsolicited to East Coast publishing houses.

★ ★ ★

THE PACKAGE MAILED to the Fifth Avenue "Editorial Department" offices of Alfred A. Knopf on February 11, 1928, began simply, "Gentlemen" and introduced "an action-detective novel for your consideration. If you don't care to publish it, will you kindly return it by express, collect." The writer went on to introduce himself: "I was a Pinkerton's National Detective Agency operative for a number of years; and, more recently, have published fiction, book reviews, verse, sketches, and so on, in twenty or twenty-five magazines."

Hammett listed nearly five lines of magazine credits, while saying nothing further about his former career as a genuine sleuth, a distinction that would become so important.

Although he was growing more accustomed to literary success, the answer Hammett received from Blanche Knopf must have been almost as exciting as his first small sale to *The Smart Set* almost six years earlier. Mrs. Knopf, in addition to publishing Langston Hughes and Carl Van Vechten with her husband, was a savvy young publisher of mysteries who knew something about the detective genre. Born the same year as Hammett, she had founded the Knopf house with Alfred, on a five-thousand-dollar loan from Alfred's father, in 1915, the year Hammett became a detective. Blanche Knopf's hand was in everything at the publishing house; in addition to editing many of its established writers, she had even designed the Knopf colophon of a leaping borzoi dog.

Mrs. Knopf felt that, apart from its "hopeless" title, Poisonville was quite publishable and they were "keen" about the manuscript except for the middle of the book, where, she said, "the violence seems piled on too heavily; so many killings on a page I believe make the reader doubt the story." Beyond publishing this book, she wondered hopefully if Hammett had further "ideas for detective stories" or even any others "under way."

In fact, he had at least one other under way and more ideas than he even could execute. In his answer, Hammett submitted a list of eight title possibilities for his "Poisonville" book, some of which were even worse: *The Poisonville Murders, The Seventeenth Murder, Murder Plus, The Willsson Matter, The City of Death, The Cleansing of Poisonville, The Black City*, and, finally, *Red Harvest*, upon which they agreed.

Hammett had piled up bodies in "Poisonville" to please the readers of *Black Mask*. But when he went back to prepare it as a novel for Mrs. Knopf, he found that she (and her editor Harry Block) wanted him to remove a number of extra corpses and at least two dynamitings, and to begin to learn to do some of his killing offstage for a book audience. Dramatically, it didn't much matter how corrupt the real Butte had been, or how graphic its violence, if the truth seemed unbelievable on the page.

As he reworked his first book he was finishing his second, *The Dain Curse*, and he told Mrs. Knopf that he even had plans for a stream-of-consciousness detective novel, in which the reader learned all the clues just as the investigator did. He considered himself "one of the few—if there are any more—moderately literate people who take the detective story seriously." Mrs. Knopf was another.

Hammett still had "a flock" of book ideas even as he began to turn his attention toward Hollywood. In April 1928 he received an inquiry from Fox Films about the rights to some of his original material, which included half a dozen stories and his first novel (still in manuscript). He cabled Mrs. Knopf for advice about his "motion picture dickering" and to keep her apprised of his climbing career.[8]

By April, he wrote her that "If . . . I make a more transient connection with Fox I'll probably let the stream-of-consciousness experiment wait awhile, sticking to the more objective and filmable forms." Wait a while it did. In June, he traveled to Los Angeles to make his pitch, staying downtown at the Alexandria, an elegant eight-story hotel with the popular Palm Court ballroom, and felt like an emerging big shot. There was even hope that Fox would commission original screenplays from him. Even though no money followed from his first meeting in Hollywood, it does not seem to have shaken his belief that movie studios would ultimately want what he had to sell. Despite the lack of a deal, he followed through on his resolution, from then on, to write books that were more "objective and filmable."

When *Red Harvest* was published in February 1929, Herbert Asbury in *The Bookman* called it "the liveliest detective story that has been published in a decade," and doubted "if even Ernest Hemingway has ever written more effective dialogue." The book was hailed by a number of reviewers for its portrait of corruption and for its starkly savvy prose. Others had a more contemplative picture of how a detective should behave, and did not wish to slog about in the underworld, even with as charismatic a guide as Hammett's Op. Nevertheless, by the end of the year, the first edition of *Red Harvest* had sold out and was optioned by a film company—not Fox, but Paramount Studios.

Six months after publication of his first novel, Knopf brought out *The Dain Curse*, in July 1929, a mystery that expands on the sinister California theme of cults built around sex and drugs that Hammett had sketched out in "The Scorched Face," only this time the Op was not searching for a rebellious "wandering daughter" but trying to save one who had been convinced she was evil, the inheritor of a false family curse. (As such a wide-ranging reader, Hammett may even have been inspired by an old Wilkie Collins story about inherited mental illness, "Mad Monkton.")

The book, which had also been serialized in *Black Mask*, was Hammett's last starring his Op. It featured a lean, "sorrel-haired" writer as a villain, drew a little on the knowledge of jewels Hammett had gained during his brief advertising career, and contained some other inside jokes about the office. It was dedicated to Albert Samuels.* Few reviewers thought it as good as *Red Harvest*, including Hammett, who later found the story "silly," but *The Dain Curse* did sell out its first three printings and was full of memorable lines from his wisecracking detective. It also gained Hammett his first review mention in the *New York Times*, as part of a Christmas roundup of books.

Hammett was now writing as well and as quickly as he ever would. By the time Knopf published *The Dain Curse*, he had already submitted his third novel, what he introduced as "by far the best thing I've done so far." After experimenting with other physical types for sleuths in some non-Op stories (including a fat, hyperbolically ugly PI named Alexander Rush), he had developed a new detective worthy of the long haul of starring in his own novel. He was taller, looked and acted a little like a "blond Satan," and answered to no one but the client—not to an Old Man of the office, not even to his business partner, for whom he showed his contempt by bedding his wife. Sam Spade was about to come snarling to life.

---

* With three of his books, *The Maltese Falcon*, *The Dain Curse*, and *The Glass Key*, the honoree got the dedication once Hammett had moved on.

Chapter XII

AMONG THE GHOSTS

*The contemporary novelist's job is to take pieces of
life and arrange them on paper. And the more direct
their passage from street to paper, the more lifelike
they should be.*

—DASHIELL HAMMETT, 1934

IF YOU GO AROUND town looking for it, you'll find boasts
that Dashiell Hammett wrote *The Maltese Falcon* in all corners
of San Francisco. At the Flood Building on Market Street,
where he worked for Pinkerton's before he ever wrote anything,
a proprietary caption accompanies the black bird on display
in the lobby; around the corner, at John's Grill on Ellis Street,
the menu reprints Fritz Lieber's "Stalking Sam Spade," and the
marker out front (HOME OF THE MALTESE FALCON) suggests he
scribbled some of his masterwork here among the beer glasses
and T-bones. (The waiters somehow all know this for a fact.)
John's Grill, with its marvelous long neon sign and three floors
decked out with *Falcon* memorabilia, has served as a headquarters for Hammett scholars over the years and earned its spot on

the to-do lists of tourists who come to order the Sam Spade Special, a dinner of "chops, baked potato, and sliced tomatoes" that Spade quickly eats there in the novel. The falcon statuette in a glass case on John's second floor is the best known of all the replicas in the city. When it was stolen in 2007, a twenty-five-thousand-dollar bounty failed to bring it back, but a replacement bird was created by art students.*

Across Ellis Street from John's, at the Hotel Union Square, where he never stayed or wrote but did put up his pregnant fiancée before their wedding in 1921, the *Thin Man* movies play quietly on a continuous loop in the lobby. Fans of the writer can sleep in the Dashiell Hammett Suite, which features a SPADE & ARCHER sign in the window, fedora and mackintosh on a coatrack, a suitcase filled with Hammett paperbacks, and framed pictures of both Hammett's wife, Jose, and his companion Lillian Hellman. (Many Hammett enthusiasts who have stayed in the suite have put the discordant Hellman portrait facedown during their stay: after all, she has nothing to do with San Francisco.) The most charming feature of the suite is the lovely chiming of the cable cars passing under the windows, on their way to and from the grinding turntable at the bottom of Powell Street. And while the literature that comes with the room claims he wrote his great San Francisco works in the 1930s (when he had gone to New York and Hollywood), still, it is a fine place to have a drink and think about Hammett.

All that's known for sure is he wrote *The Maltese Falcon* mostly in the studio he rented not that far away, at 891 Post

---

* A falcon statuette used in John Huston's 1941 movie sold at auction for four million dollars in 2013.

Street, which sits just within the Tenderloin district. He had moved there while still working as advertising manager for Albert Samuels, and it is where Sam Spade first came to life, a "hard and shifty fellow" if ever there was one. After two strong books, Hammett produced a nearly perfect one in this space of barely three hundred square feet. Unlike with his Op or the Old Man, Hammett claimed no direct inspiration for Spade from his own experience: "Spade had no original," he remembered in 1934. "He is a dream man in the sense that he is what most of the private detectives I worked with would like to have been and what quite a few of them in their cockier moments thought they approached."[1] But he and Spade shared more than that, starting with their common apartment.

He put so much of himself into Spade—gave him the rooms he was living in and the streets he knew well; added a handsome, angular face very much like his own, as well as a risky romance with a woman inspired by one he had met at the office, Peggy O'Toole; gave him a cop antagonist with the name of a boy from his old Baltimore neighborhood, Polhaus; he attached the name of a favorite cousin, Effie, to Spade's "invaluable angel" of a secretary, and then christened Spade with his own first name, which he used less and less, Sam.* The rest, of course, was a rough-edged "dream man" with yellow-gray eyes, the perfect foil for the invading throng of deadly treasure hunters chasing an antique black bird. Hammett's new mystery presented a private detective uniquely suited to his wicked world, as

---

* In fact, he could now date friends from eras of his life by which name they called him.

Hammett said, "able to get the best of anybody he comes in contact with, whether criminal, innocent by-stander or client."

Like the Continental Op, who prefers to stir things up and see what happens, Spade's "way of learning" is to "heave a wild and unpredictable monkey-wrench into the machinery." But unlike the Op, Spade is not a company man. Others have written about Spade having a personal code ("When a man's partner is killed he's supposed to do something about it"), but he is also the perfect adaptive animal for the San Francisco of the late 1920s, the end result of Allan Pinkerton's dictum about the importance of detectives assimilating with criminals. "Don't be too sure I'm as crooked as I'm supposed to be," Spade reminds Brigid O'Shaughnessy.

Sam Spade launched a thousand tough-guy sleuths, yet he remains more lifelike because he is not really knowable beyond his ruthless focus and weakness for women. Spade is given to sudden rages that might be strategic, draws a punch from a cop as a way of sounding him out ("in losing his head and slugging me he overplayed his hand"); even when he sleeps with his beautiful client, you aren't sure it isn't just to steal her key to search her room:

> At his side, Brigid O'Shaughnessy's soft breathing had the regularity of utter sleep. Spade was quiet leaving bed and bedroom and shutting bedroom-door. He dressed in the bathroom. Then he examined the sleeping girl's clothes, took a flat brass key from the pocket of her coat, and went out.[2]

He examines every crevice of Brigid's hotel suite, then returns to cheerfully make her breakfast. He crosses so many lines and mostly crosses back, keeping cop and crook off balance, a quality that allows him to play each of the falcon hunters off the others. But as a wise lady once said to the Hammett authority Don Herron as he was leading one of his Hammett tours, you don't know how the book might turn out if Spade held a real, bejeweled falcon in his hands.

Inside Hammett's small Post Street studio, you can easily imagine Spade rolling his cigarettes and jauntily serving Bacardi to his unwelcome guests. According to the Friends of Libraries plaque placed on the wall of the apartment building in 2005, DASHIELL HAMMETT LIVED IN THIS BUILDING FROM 1926 UNTIL 1929, WHEN HE WROTE HIS FIRST THREE NOVELS. Several of those months were spent elsewhere, but as the inscription continues, this space is also significant as the home of Sam Spade: MODELED ON HAMMETT'S, ON THE NORTHWEST CORNER OF THE FOURTH FLOOR.

An original member of the Maltese Falcon Society, Don Herron has helped thousands along the Hammett trail since founding his Dashiell Hammett Tour in 1977. Hammett transformed himself while living in San Francisco, and Herron, born in Detroit, also became the man he is only after moving here, during the city's scruffier prime, long before tech money raised the rents and Google buses prowled the streets.

Herron has been climbing the San Francisco hillsides since the Jimmy Carter era on behalf of the enthusiasts who show up on designated Sundays, cash in hand, to follow this tall bearded man in his comfortable trench coat: throngs of actors, English professors, Bogie fans, hard-boiled know-it-alls, and kindly buffs. He has led groups of amateur sleuths (from the Mystery Writers of America) as well as professional detectives, and he had the honor of bringing the writer's daughter Jo Hammett full circle back to her first childhood home on Eddy Street and to the Post Street studio with the cramped elevator where her father wrote *The Maltese Falcon*.

After a short, close elevator ride, the apartment door opens into a curved passageway with a recessed wooden phone box of the kind once used for buzzing in guests. On the other side of the wall from the phone is a small but bright kitchen, while in the main room, a Murphy bed is folded away behind a door ("In his bedroom that was a living room now the wall bed was up . . ."). Against the wall a period desk sits beneath a framed map of San Francisco, with a solid black Royal typewriter on a leather blotter, and behind the typewriter stands another falcon.

Turning right from the desk there is a long window view down Post Street, for whenever the writer needed to look away from the "swell lot of thieves" of his imagination. A Gramophone sits on its stand in the corner, opposite a glass-fronted bookcase. Hanging over the scene is an acorn-shaped alabaster light fixture, a little more sculptural than the plain "white bowl, hung on three gilded chains" that lights Spade's room in the novel. Missing also is the sound of the old Alcatraz foghorn's "dull moaning" through Spade's open windows.

Starting with Sergeant Polhaus, almost every major character comes to Sam's apartment to harass him at some point in the novel, wanting him for murder or love or treasure. One can imagine the bulbous villain Casper Gutman seated heavily on the room's couch discussing the history of his black bird, or Brigid O'Shaughnessy undressing in Sam's bathroom to prove she's not a thief.

Young Sam Hammett in his parents' backyard on North Stricker Street in Baltimore, just before leaving the Pinkertons for the Army in 1918. (Julie M. Rivett)

"Dearest Woman," Josephine Annis Dolan (called Jose), met Sam Hammett when he was brought to the Cushman Institute in the fall of 1920. (Julie M. Rivett)

Transferred for his health, the smitten young lung patient has a smoke outside San Diego, 1921. (Julie M. Rivett)

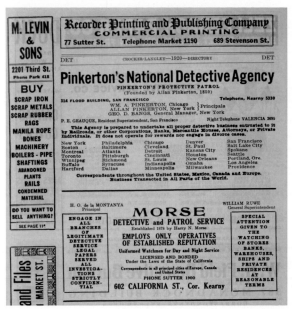

M. LEVIN & SONS

2201 Third St.
Phone Park 412

BUY
SCRAP IRON
SCRAP METALS
SCRAP RUBBER
RAGS
MANILA ROPE
BONES
MACHINERY
BOILERS - PIPE
SHAFTINGS
ABANDONED
PLANTS
RAILS
CONDEMNED
MATERIAL

DO YOU WANT TO
SELL ANYTHING?
SEE PAGE 11*

and Files   MARKET ST.

Advertisement for Pinkerton's San Francisco office, 1920, with Hammett's supervisor, Phil Geauque, the future Secret Service man, on the masthead. (Internet Archive)

San Francisco's James Flood Building on Market Street near the cable-car turnaround on Powell. Pinkerton's had room 314. (San Francisco History Center, San Francisco Public Library)

The renowned Pinkerton detective James McParland probably inspired the Continental Agency's Old Man ("A tall, plump man in his seventies . . . with a white-mustached, baby-pink, grandfatherly face, mild blue eyes behind rimless spectacles"), as well as a character in a late Sherlock Holmes novel. (Library of Congress)

Tough guy in transition: the ex-detective and emerging artist lights a match on the rooftop of the Crawford Apartments on Eddy Street in San Francisco, August 10, 1925. (Julie M. Rivett)

The natty young father sitting with daughter Mary in approximately the same year, 1925, with San Francisco stretching wide-open behind them (Julie M. Rivett)

Hammett looking gaunt yet determined in a Morris chair at the Crawford Apartments, early 1920s (Julie M. Rivett)

Red Harvest featured a fictional rendering of Butte, Montana, "an ugly city . . . set in an ugly notch between two ugly mountains that had been all dirtied up by mining." (Random House)

Jose, Mary, and Jo sent Hammett this haunting snapshot from Montana during their months-long separation around 1926. (Julie M. Rivett)

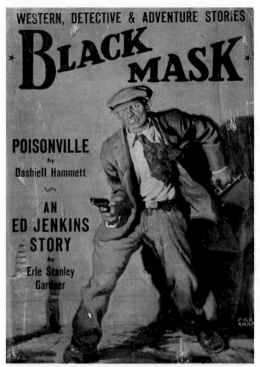

The cover for the Continental Op adventure that became *Red Harvest*: "The Cleansing of Poisonville," in the September 1927 issue of *Black Mask* (Layman Hammett Collection, Irvin Department of Rare Books and Special Collections, University of South Carolina Libraries, Columbia, S.C.)

H. C. Murphy's cool-under-fire cover image for the September 1929 issue of *Black Mask* was the definitive picture of Sam Spade until John Huston's 1941 movie. (Layman Hammett Collection, Irvin Department of Rare Books and Special Collections, University of South Carolina Libraries, Columbia, S.C.)

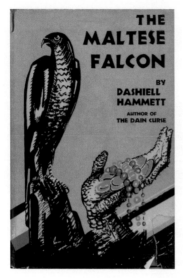

When the novel was first published in February 1930, Gilbert Seldes wrote in the *New York Graphic*, "The detectives of fiction have been knocked into a cocked hat . . . by the appearance of Sam Spade in a book called *The Maltese Falcon.*" (Random House)

The maestro at his keyboard: Hammett is pictured in his writing prime for a newspaper profile, 1934. (Harry Ransom Collection)

After Hammett left it in 1929,[*] tenant after tenant occupied his small studio at 891 Post, presumably unaware of its possible literary significance. Then, more than six decades later, Bill Arney moved in among the Hammett ghosts and began his architectural detective work.

Arney first saw the outside of Post Street while taking Don Herron's tour in July 1982. Eleven years later, he recognized the building as he passed it in a cab, with a For Rent sign outside: apartment 401 was available. Arney had heard this was Hammett's apartment number from Herron, who got it from the novelist Joe Gores, who cited the *Crocker-Langley San Francisco City Directory*. But Hammett had never said his old apartment definitely belonged to Sam Spade. The man Don Herron calls the "pivotal tenant" ultimately made the case that Hammett's and Spade's apartments were one and the same.

Arney's discovery of the apartment would take him deep inside the Hammett cult as he lived with Sam Spade for fourteen years. "I did not know for sure that it was *really* Spade's apartment until I sat in there and read the novel," Arney recalls. "Now, *that* was spooky. For the first months, it was *incredibly* spooky, to the point where it was hard to get to sleep at night."[3]

Arney noticed that his apartment had a bend and a small closet in the front passageway, just like Sam's, and that there was a door between the passageway and the main room, which few other units in the building had. When the cops visit Sam's place the night of Archer's murder, Spade hears the elevator cage

---

[*] Although the city directory has him living at 1155 Leavenworth in 1928-29, he continued to write letters from 891 Post Street right up until he left town in October 1929.

door rattling open. In those days, the apartment door was glass, therefore less soundproof, like the door between the passageway and the living room/bedroom, which Arney rescued from the basement. The bathroom's layout also accommodated the famous strip search later in the novel, allowing Brigid to take off her clothes without being between the bathtub and the toilet (where Sam lays the pistols) or between the bathtub and the door. This keeps her discreetly out of sight of Casper Gutman and others in the adjoining room.

Sam's kitchen has a breakfast nook, which Hammett's did not (none in the building did), but Arney theorized that Hammett added the nook to the novel to accommodate certain scenes between Sam and Brigid. As he escorts Brigid into the bathroom, Spade warns his other guests, "unless you want a three-story drop, there's no way out of here except past the bathroom door." While many of the studio's features were shared by others on that side of the building, that line put Sam's place clearly on the fourth floor.

Once he was convinced, Arney began letting Herron bring tours through his place on Sunday afternoons. He now lived inside a novel, a masterpiece, but a novel just the same—with Brigid O'Shaughnessy on his couch and in his bathroom, Sam's bed in the wall, police detectives in his hallway, the Levantine treasure hunter Joel Cairo worrying in his rocker, and Casper Gutman pontificating on a padded chair. His home became a pilgrimage, and toward the end of his tenure, he was putting himself to sleep listening to old radio recordings of "The Adventures of Sam Spade." After fourteen years of hosting, Arney got married and moved to a larger place, one less freighted with literary meaning, but he held on to apartment

401 for two more years, hoping to safely hand over the small museum he had built.

The Hammett aficionado and founder of the Noir City Film Festival, Eddie Muller, got Arney in touch with a writer and philanthropist from Pacific Heights, Robert Mailer Anderson, who acquired the lease and turned a decorator loose in the place. Despite some glamorous touches, if the studio were clouded with a little Fatima smoke, it might seem Hammett had just left the room.

In *The Maltese Falcon*, Hammett presents Spade whole and unexplained, without a word about his past except the famous "Flitcraft Parable" Sam tells Brigid, about a man he once hunted in the Northwest. Writers have long puzzled over the inclusion of the Flitcraft story in the novel, a kind of extra pearl in an already sparkling necklace, and John Huston understandably left it out of his otherwise faithful movie version. Although every possible meaning has been gleaned from Hammett's story by scholars, there seems little mystery about where he found this character's name. During Hammett's Pinkerton days, detectives working on insurance cases would consult a life insurance manual put out annually by a publisher in Oak Park, Illinois named Allen J. Flitcraft. Hammett, favoring the in-joke, later borrowed Flitcraft's name for his parable.*

---

* The novelist Joe Gores pointed out (in his introduction to *Lost Stories*) that the name Flitcraft refers to a book of "actuarial tables" known to all private detectives in Hammett's time. Pinkerton's (as well as the fictional Continental Agency) had sizable insurance companies for clients. The *A. J. Flitcraft Life Insurance Manual* from 1918, which Hammett presumably consulted, has since become available online. It seems more likely that he plucked this name from

As Spade tells it to Brigid, a young real estate executive named Charles Flitcraft was on his lunch hour one day in Tacoma in the early 1920s when he was nearly killed by a beam that fell from a construction site and crashed beside him on the sidewalk, a piece of concrete even nicking his face to emphasize how close to death he had come. Shaken by his near miss, Flitcraft spontaneously left his family, drifted to San Francisco, and eventually resettled in Spokane. Five years after the disappearance, Sam Spade, then working out of "one of the big detective agencies in Seattle" (as Hammett had), was hired by Mrs. Flitcraft to find her lost husband, whom she had heard might be in Spokane (where Hammett had also worked). He located the unrepentant Flitcraft in that city, where the missing husband had begun a whole new family and career under a new name. He explained to Sam the reasonableness of his reaction to his close call with the crashing beam:

> "He was scared stiff, of course, but he was more shocked than really frightened. He felt like somebody had taken the lid off life and let him look at the works."

Flitcraft had left his first family well provided for, he tells Spade,

and what he had done seemed to him perfectly reasonable. The only thing that bothered him was a doubt that he could

---

the manual to amuse himself than that he was referring to obscure philosophers of flux, as some suggest, but the debate over the "Flitcraft Parable" will go on, because it is a mesmerizing piece of writing worth staring into.

make that reasonableness clear to Spade. He had never told anybody his story before, and thus had not had to make its reasonableness explicit. He tried now.

"I got it all right," Spade told Brigid O'Shaughnessy, "but Mrs. Flitcraft never did. She thought it was silly. Maybe it was."

The Sam Spade of the rest of the novel might have hauled the errant husband by his ear back to Seattle to have him explain himself to Mrs. Flitcraft in person. She was the client, after all. In some ways it is a reworking of an earlier missing husband story, the sound-alike Norman Ashcraft in "The Golden Horseshoe," relentlessly pursued by the Op on the wife's behalf, even after she is dead.

But Spade's reaction to the story Flitcraft tells him is muted and surprising; there is something deeper going on. As he wrote this, Hammett had been living apart from his own family off and on for several years, and was considering making the separation complete by moving three thousand miles away, to New York. He had come to the Post Street studio on orders to shield his young children from his TB, and, once living apart, found the solitude and freedom that, among other things, allowed him to become a novelist. As he finished the manuscript of *The Maltese Falcon*, Hammett had survived a full decade with a disease that might have killed him at anytime, an experience that had certainly lifted the lid off life and showed him the works.

Flitcraft's is a far colder, cleaner departure than Hammett's gradual separation, but his story feels mysteriously charged as Spade tells it, because Hammett, a man between lives, is talking to himself through his creation. He had tried living at home, and living away from home, and had adjusted to his new life. The fact that he could not return to his old life might seem unreasonable to others, but there it was.

If tuberculosis laid him low and forced him to find his way to a writing career, its later diminution allowed him a chance to roam. He convinced Jose to move the girls to Los Angeles, where some of her Kelly relatives wintered and where he felt his movie prospects might take him sometime in the future. If Jose took care of the girls, he promised, he would take care of her.

He departed San Francisco altogether in early October 1929, along with a woman named Nell Martin and a generous send-off loan of five hundred dollars from his fond ex-employer Albert Samuels. They arrived in New York just ahead of the great stock market crash. It somehow fits with Hammett's biography that, having spent much of the Roaring Twenties sick and impoverished, his fate would again zig when the rest of the country zagged.

Nell Martin is sometimes described simply as a widowed music teacher and actress but in fact listed herself as divorced and was, by this time, the author of many stories, light mysteries and satires, including the novels *The Mosaic Earring*, *Lord Byron of Broadway*, and *The Constant Simp*. She was a witty survivor who had held an even wider variety of jobs than Hammett had, including working as a newspaper reporter and migrant worker and driving a taxi in Chicago. She had a movie adaptation of one of her novels in production and shared Hammett's interest in the new field of screenwriting that the talkies made possible. The pair went to New York, where they stayed in an apartment in the east Thirties, from which he snapped street scenes to send his daughters.* Hammett worked there to finish his next novel, *The Glass Key*, which he would gratefully dedicate to Nell Martin after they had dissolved as a couple; she returned the gesture with her next book, cheekily titled *Lovers Should Marry*.

Hammett had arrived in New York just as the first installment of *The Maltese Falcon* triumphantly ran in *Black Mask*, announced by editor Cap Shaw as the greatest detective fiction to appear in any magazine he had ever read. When the novel was published by Knopf in February 1930, Gilbert Seldes in the *New York Graphic* wrote, "The detectives of fiction have been knocked into a cocked hat . . . by the appearance of Sam Spade in a book called *The Maltese Falcon*." "The horsepower of Mr. Hammett's pen," said the *New York Herald Tribune*, "must be sampled to be believed." The novel would be reprinted seven times in a year. It wasn't, however, dedicated to Nell Martin but to Josephine Hammett ("To Jose"), the steadfast woman he had left behind, at least for now. As consolation, their daughter Jo Hammett pointed out, her mother got the best book.

---

* There is scholarly confusion about their romance: the 1930 federal census lists one Nell Martin, "writer," at 133 East Thirty-Eighth Street, a "divorced" "head of household" living with two other women as "lodgers." Hammett would move in with her at Thirty-Eighth Street for a time after he returned to New York from a stint in Hollywood in 1931.

Chapter XIII

BABYLON AND BACK

"I was fascinated by him," Dorothy said, meaning
me, "a real live detective, and used to follow him
around making him tell me about his experiences.
He told me awful lies, but I believed every word."

—*The Thin Man*

THINGS SEEMED TO be happening for him all at once
when Hammett arrived in Manhattan: he finally met
the Knopfs while overseeing the publication of *The Maltese
Falcon*, and made the circuit sporting the look that would
become increasingly familiar, as his reputation grew, of the lean,
striking-looking ex-detective seen across the room at parties or
nightclubs, with his brush of white hair and flecked mustache,
tweed suits, and affecting a cane on the street. He also had
a movie option for *Red Harvest* from Paramount.[1] While
Hammett's first residency in New York was action packed, he
somehow also completed his superb fourth novel, set largely in a
hard city resembling his old Baltimore.

In later years, when he struggled to complete book projects, he would blame his diminished output on the psychic cost of one marathon session of thirty straight hours writing *The Glass Key*, finishing the last third of the novel in the fall of 1929. Although he credited this binge of creativity for his decline, it was less likely that this writing session had burned it out of him than all the other nights spent bingeing on everything else; or, for that matter, the driving pace at which he had turned out his first four novels, uncertain when the TB might return and take him. If *The Maltese Falcon* was "the best detective story America has yet produced," as Alexander Woollcott called it, *The Glass Key* was Hammett's last great book. It remained his favorite.

It might have started out as an underworld novel about a gunman. At the end of a list of possible projects he had sent his Knopf editor, Harry Block, back in June, Hammett confided, "I had intended doing the story of a gunman next, but, according to [Herbert] Asbury, *Little Caesar* was that. So until I've read it, I'm holding off."[2] W. R. Burnett's powerful gangster novel seemed to make quite an impression in the meantime. If *The Glass Key* began life as an idea for a novel about a gunman, he later elevated the plot and characters to something more complex.

In the book, a lean, tubercular gambler and "politician's hanger-on" named Ned Beaumont discovers the body of the playboy son of a senator lying in the dark street and alerts his boss and friend, the powerful ward heeler Paul Madvig. On a weeks-long losing gambling streak, Beaumont borrows money from Madvig that he bets on a horse named Peggy O'Toole, and then goes chasing after his winnings when his bookie absconds to New York with his $3,200. Ned's interest in who killed the senator's son and the election strategy for Paul Madvig's slate of candidates are complicated by Madvig's designs to marry the senator's daughter—a desire that throws Madvig off his political game as the election nears. Ned finds himself giving Madvig counsel on both political and romantic decisions, and even unsolicited fashion advice against wearing silk socks with tweed. Beneath the surface of the political-crime plot, a love triangle threatens.

Madvig's political war with the town's chief bootlegger, Shad O'Rory, has been conducted mostly by proxy, through Madvig's functionaries on one side and O'Rory's bought news reporters on the other, until it becomes violently flushed into the open by the murder case. At one point the stoic, Hammettish Ned Beaumont, brushing his mustache with a thumbnail, meets the mobster O'Rory, a slim young man of around thirty-four (Hammett's own age) with prematurely "sleek white hair." O'Rory traps Beaumont and hands him over to his apish torturer, who beats him for days. Yet Beaumont is prized not just for his political savvy but also his loyal ability to withstand pain. "I can stand anything I've got to stand,"[3] he says early on, and his days with O'Rory's henchmen gruesomely prove it.

When he emerges from the hospital, he joins up with the senator's daughter, Janet Henry, to solve her brother's murder, in which the prime suspect has become Paul Madvig, threatening his slate's reelection, most of whom want to arrest him but lack the guts. Although *The Glass Key* is an impressive portrait of machine politicians and Prohibition mobsters, Ned Beaumont turns into a very able detective along the way. The end of the novel, perhaps written during that marathon session after Hammett first arrived from San Francisco, has Beaumont packing his bags to move to New York for good. It's the only solution for him. In an uncommonly hopeful moment in a tough book, Janet Henry goes with him.

During his months in Manhattan, Hammett collected reviews and fans for his work, from Alexander Woollcott to Dorothy Parker. But perhaps most influential for Hammett was a memo David O. Selznick wrote to his boss at Paramount Pictures, B. P. Schulberg, in July 1930. His letter came three weeks after movie rights to *The Maltese Falcon* had been bought by rival Warner Brothers for $8,500, of which Hammett kept 80 percent.[4] Paramount had released its adaptation of *Red Harvest*, called *Roadhouse Nights*, in February. Selznick now urged his boss to further "secure" Hammett, whose "vogue is on the rise" and who "might very well prove to be the creator of something new and startlingly original for us." Selznick recommended signing the former Pinkerton man to write a "police story" for the actor George Bancroft. Hammett, he approvingly noted, "is unspoiled as to money."[5]

Hammett had not been pleased with what Paramount did with *Red Harvest*, his portrait of a Western nightmare town convulsing in violence entirely softened and rewritten and featuring performances by Jimmy Durante. "They changed everything but the title," Hammett recalled, "and finally they changed that to 'Roadhouse Nights.'"

Despite this treatment, Hammett may have assumed he would have greater influence by working on his future screenplays himself, in person, or (at three hundred dollars per week with a five-thousand-dollar option for any original story accepted) perhaps the money was simply too tempting. He answered the call to Hollywood, as so many writers were then doing to gather up absurd amounts of promised cash and to hide from the deepening hard times. He could briefly visit his family before starting work for Paramount. While living at the

Hollywood Knickerbocker, he corrected proofs for *The Glass Key*, about which there was some growing film interest as well.

Outwardly, his life seemed to veer out of his control during this first time working in Hollywood, yet Hammett proved surprisingly successful when he could show up in shape to work. He wrote his first assignment (a seven-page treatment titled "After School") in a weekend, a story that was expanded as "The Kiss-Off" and ultimately produced the next year as a gangster film called *City Streets*, starring Sylvia Sidney and a young Gary Cooper, for which Hammett received a screen credit. He did various script doctoring projects, meeting William Powell, a charming, hard-drinking actor who would later reunite with Hammett for the *Thin Man* films, and the German actress Marlene Dietrich, who proved in that year's *Blonde Venus* that she could mesmerize even while clad mostly in a gorilla suit. Outside of work, there were dinners with young actresses at the Brown Derby or Chasen's (with its rack of lamb for two), fights at the Olympic Gardens, music at the Clover Club.

With his chauffeur "Jones" and some friends, Hammett traveled to San Francisco to repay Albert Samuels the loan his former boss had made to finance the move to New York the year before; after a week-long party at the Fairmont Hotel, Hammett found he needed to borrow eight hundred dollars more from Samuels, to settle up and make the return trip to Los Angeles.

He was coming off another long drinking jag when he went to a party at Daryl Zanuck's house in Hollywood one night in late November 1930. Zanuck had bought rights to *The Maltese Falcon* for Warner Brothers in July (spurring the invitation from Selznick and Paramount that had brought Hammett to Hollywood). In addition, Zanuck and Warner's were pioneering

the gangster film, having just made *Little Caesar* (with Edward
G. Robinson) and with *The Public Enemy* (starring James Cagney)
due out in the spring. These were films closer to the *Black Mask*
style of crime writing.

The party became noteworthy for Hammett for someone
else he got to know that night: a young married script reader
for MGM named Lillian Kober.* Her family name had been
Hellman, she was Jewish, opinionated and literary, had lived in
New Orleans and New York and tended toward feisty pronouncements, was odd-looking but confident, and nicely dressed with
reddish brown hair. They left the party together and carried their
drunken discussion out into Hammett's chauffeured car.

He was thirty-six and, she recalled, professionally the hottest
thing on both coasts. She was twenty-four, tepidly married to a
New York humorist and scenario writer named Arthur Kober,
and unpublished except for a few stories in a Parisian journal
edited by her husband. Hammett's "five-day drunk had left the
wonderful face looking rumpled," Hellman would remember
in *An Unfinished Woman*, "and the very tall, thin figure was
tired and sagged. We talked of T. S. Eliot, although I no longer
remember what we said, and then went and sat in his car and
talked at each other and over each other until it was daylight."[6]

---

* They could have met or noticed each other briefly at other Hollywood
gatherings before their fateful evening. While Hellman and Diane Johnson
(*Dashiell Hammett: A Life*) put the introduction at Musso and Frank restaurant
on Hollywood Boulevard, Richard Layman, writing seventeen years later in
the *Selected Letters*, defies his own 1983 biography (which defers to Hellman's
memoir) and puts it confidently at the Zanuck party. Chances are they at least
glimpsed each other before this, since they traveled in the same circle of
friends and Hammett knew Hellman's husband.

Soon he was writing verse for her. By the next year, she would be divorced and living off and on with Hammett.

Hammett parted ways with Paramount by the end of 1930. Daryl Zanuck, at Warner's, which was already making the first of three film versions of *The Maltese Falcon*, commissioned Hammett in January 1931 to write a new Sam Spade story for William Powell. The actor had also just come over to Warner and previously played the gentlemanly detective Philo Vance, the highly popular book series character by S. S. Van Dine whom Hammett had disparaged in print as a "bore" who was always wrong. Hammett's deal with Warner's was worth fifteen thousand dollars, to be paid in three installments, upon approval.[7]

For the rest of the country, the year 1931 was a time of nearly 20 percent unemployment, bank panics, and hundreds of failures as a recession hardened into depression. New York's Bank of the United States had gone under the year before, the largest failure in the country's history, and newspapers published advice on how smaller banks could stave off runs by fearful depositors: managers in Chicago had rushed in a jazz band to distract panicked customers, while in Raleigh they gave out coffee and sandwiches to quiet them; one savings and loan put out an open valise full of thousand-dollar bills as a calming display of fiscal health. Hollywood, as usual, felt far from all of that.[8]

Hammett's daughters visited him during his time in Hollywood, sometimes encountering worldly young ladies before going out to shop nearby at Brock's jewelers or eat lunch at the Brown Derby with their glamorous screenwriter father. "We caught glimpses of a different world when we visited him," wrote Jo Hammett. "The light had a golden feel; things smelled different."[9] At such times, Hammett's life must have seemed almost as he'd pictured it when he first convinced Jose to move to Los Angeles anticipating his success in the movies. Sometimes a box of chocolates would come home with the girls for Jose, or a carved box picked out with the help of one of his young ladies, and he continued to write her fond letters. The couple remained married, and he kept to his promise by sending her checks, faithfully if not always predictably.

After two rounds (and ten thousand dollars), Hammett's screen treatment "On the Make" was ultimately rejected by Warner's that April.* In his letter, Zanuck explained that what had been commissioned as a Sam Spade story had "none of the qualifications of *Maltese Falcon.*" The Warner Brothers adaptation of the novel, released later in 1931 with Ricardo Cortez as Spade, suffered by comparison as well.

For Hammett, his boozy months in Los Angeles were punctuated by frantic cables to his patient publisher Alfred Knopf, asking for money (IN DESPERATE NEED OF ALL MONEY I CAN FIND). He caught his third case of gonorrhea during this time and, when Lillian Hellman had to leave town to visit New York in March, feathered his letters to her with accounts of his runs to the toilet. A month later he wrote that he was still "out of commission" but couldn't keep from "pimping" for friends such as the New York humorist Sid (S. J.) Perelman, in Hollywood with his wife, Laura, trying to write screenplays. (Laura Perelman's dog Asta would later give its name to the

---

* The rights reverted to Hammett, who later sold the screenplay to Universal, where, once the main character was renamed with the initials T.N.T., it was reborn as *Mister Dynamite* in 1935. In an influential lawsuit later brought by Warner's over ownership of the *Falcon* characters, Hammett prevailed.

famous schnauzer* sidekick of Nick and Nora Charles in *The Thin Man*.)

"Something's got to be done to keep the gals moderately content while I'm out of order," Hammett told Hellman. Such drunken letters were no doubt meant to manipulate a swift return by his new lover, but they mostly sketched a gamey picture of life in Hollywood. When he surmised that Hellman had been with another man, he proudly called her a "she-Hammett." "Alcohol has had me pretty much out of touch," Hammett explained in another letter from April 1931, when he also wrote Alfred Knopf, "I think *The Thin Man* will be my last detective novel." Most of it did not yet exist.

Normally reticent, he could become animated and then famously mean as he drank. There were occasional incidents—a knife throwing at a party where he'd seemed to be enjoying himself earlier—and worse, according to one young actress he had seen for a time, Elise De Viane, who sued him for battery and attempted rape after an evening in his hotel room. Hammett would not appear in court to contest the charge and lost a civil settlement of $2,500 in 1932. Whatever occurred, Hammett had scared himself enough to stop drinking for a while, unable to sell a screen treatment on one coast or deliver a novel on the other. According to friends, he had another collapse. In August 1931, Alfred Knopf deposited the money in the Irving Trust that Hammett said he desperately needed in order to come back to New York, then he closed his telegram to his author, LOOKING FORWARD EAGERLY SEEING YOU AND RECEIVING THIN MAN.[10]

---

* While originally a schnauzer in the novel, Asta became a white terrier in the *Thin Man* films.

He had gone to Hollywood at the height of his creative powers and learned just what he was capable of with the money Hollywood had thrown at him, money he had giddily, contemptuously, tossed away. By the time he returned to New York in September 1931, it could no longer be said that he was "unspoiled as to money."

★ ★ ★

DURING THE WINTER of 1932, Sid Perelman saw Hammett back in New York, at the Sutton Club Hotel on East Fifty-Sixth Street. To land there, Hammett had burned through his remaining movie money at more luxurious establishments, living lushly at the Hotel Elysée and the Biltmore and the Hotel Pierre on Fifth Avenue, where he was finally stranded in his suite, unable to settle his bill of a thousand dollars. Word reached his friends, who invited him to join the group of literary guests (James T. Farrell, Erskine Caldwell, Herbert Asbury) living cheaply at the nearby Sutton, a good place to work if you were close to broke and didn't care, for the time being, about ugly furniture or bad coffee.

Hammett contrived a scheme for sneaking out on his bill at the Pierre: "His knowledge of the mentality of house detectives provided the key," Sid Perelman recalled in a memoir. "Hammett decided to use fat as a subterfuge. He pulled on four shirts, three suits, innumerable socks, two lightweight ulsters, and an overcoat, cramming his pockets with assorted toiletries. Then he puffed out his cheeks, strode past the desk without a glimmer of suspicion, and headed for the Sutton." There, when the faux fat man arrived, Perelman and others were all gratefully ensconced with their own projects. Hammett brought his own.

The Sutton Club was a serviceable new establishment managed by Sid Perelman's brother-in-law, Nathanael "Pep" West, who offered his empty rooms to a clientele of deserving writers. Ability to pay was not the main criterion for West in sneaking in his literary guests in his unofficial writer's colony. West himself had so far written one unpublishable novella, and was working on his first short masterpiece, *Miss Lonelyhearts*, about a newspaper advice columnist with a Christ complex, which Hammett would read in manuscript while a guest at the hotel. West put three grubby rooms together for Hammett and classily dubbed it the Diplomatic Suite. Hammett would stay eight crucial months.[11]

Before the move, he had written "A Man Called Spade" for *American Magazine*—he did three high-paying Spade stories in 1932—and a cinematic novella called *Woman in the Dark* was serialized in *Liberty*. Now he was primed to push on with the final novel he would ever publish, completed in a flourish of surprising discipline, given how wildly he had been living. Lillian Hellman recalled him pounding away in his shabby suite:

> I had known Dash when he was writing short stories, but I had never been around for a long piece of work: The drinking stopped, the parties were over. The locking-in time had come and nothing was allowed to disturb it until the book was finished. I had never seen anybody work that way: the care for every word, the pride in the neatness of the typed page itself, the refusal for ten days or two weeks to go out for even a walk for fear something would be lost.[12]

He may not have feared only that something would be lost, but, given how things had unraveled on the West Coast, that something already had been. But, in an impressive last stand, he finished the book, against which he had already borrowed several times from Knopf. It was not his best work, but it would become his most popular, especially in combination with the series of films it inspired.

He had spent eight comparatively spartan months at the Sutton. After pulling the final page from his typewriter and turning in the manuscript in the spring of 1933, he was back briefly in the black, and the time for "locking-in" and discipline was over. Liquor was again legal.

The book he had written, in addition to its central mystery plot about the search for a missing inventor, Clyde Wynant, over several days in December, was also clearly an account of what it was like to be suddenly wealthy and an ex-detective from San Francisco, spending as quickly as the money came in and bantering with your sophisticated lady friend at a series of parties and Manhattan hotels.

Sometimes in his bathrobe, having scotch for breakfast, Nick Charles is a burnt-out case moved to do things mainly out of love for his wife. "We didn't come to New York to stay sober," he reminds her when events threaten his Christmas plans. Up from the lobby of his Hotel Normandie come a host of characters from his detecting past. The adventure seeks him out, buzzed and resistant as he is. Even when wounded by a bullet, he is in his hotel bed, throwing a pillow in defense. Nick Charles is three things rare in a good detective: drunk, famous, and accompanied usually by his charming wife.

Nothing about *The Thin Man* seems especially dangerous, just as its protagonist is retired from the active line of fire himself. The comedic mystery was new when Hammett produced his final published novel, which opens with Nick waiting in a Fifty-Second Street speakeasy while Nora shops at Saks and Lord &

Taylor with the dog. The Charleses are too sophisticated for a classic suspense story.

> "Listen, Mac, I haven't been a detective for six years, since 1927." He stared at me. "On the level," I assured him, "a year after I got married, my wife's father died and left her a lumber mill and a narrow-gauge railroad and some other things and I quit the Agency to look after them."[13]

As witty as its characters are, *The Thin Man* has an undercurrent of sadness beneath its partying façade. It is a novel whose larger setting is fame. Nick Charles, like Hammett, seems a bit adrift in New York society, the more so because people he meets admire him for things he did in a harder life years ago. He does love calling for the newspapers to be sent up to the couple's hotel room, to see how reporters have written him up. Recovering from the last bleary months, typing in his cheap rooms at the Sutton, Hammett wrote about fancy hotels and wealthy women and being newly famous. Nora was Lillian, he told her, but then she was also the crazy young blonde and the "villainess," too. He dedicated the book "To Lillian."

The novel's false start, the original sixty-five pages he wrote and abandoned in 1930, had been set in San Francisco, with a darker plot and more conventional detective and a tubercular writer as the killer. When Knopf delayed *The Glass Key* from fall to spring publication, Hammett put this new manuscript aside. By the time he returned to the book, he moved the action east and made it about an ex-detective on vacation with his heiress wife in New York when a crime comes to his attention that demands a few of the skills from his old days at the Transcontinental Detective Agency in San Francisco. Nora insists he investigate; otherwise, he would stay retired.

Knopf published *The Thin Man* in January 1934, and it was quickly sold to MGM for twenty-one thousand dollars. The first chapters had actually made the magazine rounds without a bite for several months—turned down by one editor after another over the book's apparent hard-drinking lewdness and amorality—before *Redbook* bought the rights for twenty-six thousand dollars and ran it in December 1933. The magazine exercised its right to expurgate, making one deleted exchange infamous and central to Knopf's winking advertisement in the *Times*: "Twenty thousand people don't buy a book within three weeks to read a five-word question." The deleted "question on page 192" was Nora's: "Tell me something, Nick. Tell me the truth: when you were wrestling with Mimi, didn't you have an erection?"

Having an urbane pair of highballing sleuths who solve mysteries accompanied by their schnauzer wouldn't have quite fit in the rugged, action-driven *Black Mask*, where Hammett built his name. Nick Charles in his new society life was about as much a detective anymore as Hammett himself. *The Glass Key* had been a gritty Depression-era book; *The Thin Man* was an escape story for hard times, a lighter kind of mystery that had not been tried before, told by a recognizably cynical narrator who only recently became one of the swells. It proved an enormous hit.*

In February 1934, just after Knopf published *The Thin Man*, Hammett and Hellman headed south to spend four days in

---

* The last of the six *Thin Man* films came out in 1947.

Miami. While drinking one night with his friend the screen-writer Nunnally Johnson, Hammett even managed to get himself arrested for tossing concrete rubble through a window of a Burdine's department store. "I hate Burdine's," he explained to Johnson, who raised his bail.

From Miami, he and Hellman traveled forty miles down the Keys, to a fishing camp on Key Largo. "The place I am now is an island off the coast of Florida, with coconut trees and all sorts of things," he wrote his daughters. "Yesterday I went fishing out in the Atlantic trying to catch a sailfish, which is about seven feet long . . . [A]ll I caught was a grouper (a fat ugly fish that looks something like a catfish) and a couple of barracuda, which are fish with great big teeth like dogs." He and Hellman stayed a happy few weeks fishing, swimming, reading, and (despite sober declarations in his letters) almost certainly drinking. He told his daughters he was going to bed each night at ten and rising at six, was "as sunburned as a Zulu," and "feeling better than I have felt for years."[14]

It may have been one of the happier times of his life, with a new book selling well and a movie adaptation opening soon; a Modern Library edition of *The Maltese Falcon* due in bookstores and his own comic strip that he scripted (at least at first), *Secret Agent X9*, running with great fanfare in Hearst papers since January. After some hard years, there was almost more money coming in than he could throw away. When he returned north that June, to New York, the *Thin Man* movie had opened, starring Myrna Loy and William Powell as Nick and Nora Charles, clinking glasses and hurling boozy repartee much like his own imagined banter with Hellman. In time he would come to despise his two creations, writing to Hellman that "nobody ever invented a more insufferably smug pair of characters," but the first *Thin Man* film opened with Hammett's surprised blessing. Riding the train from New York to Los Angeles, he sent off a cable to Lillian from Kansas City and signed it "Nicky." The year he turned forty was as fine as any he had had.

By October 1934, his new franchise had brought him back to Hollywood, where, after the *Thin Man* movie had proved so surprisingly popular with audiences and critics, a sequel was expected. The executives at MGM, conceding that Hammett was crucial to the sensibility of its hit film, lured him back west at two thousand dollars per week while he finished a new screen story, but stipulating that he obey all "reasonable" studio regulations as he worked. Once ensconced again in Hollywood, he wrote a short mea culpa to Alfred Knopf, who was looking forward to seeing his contracted sixth novel:

Dear Alfred—

So I'm a bum—so what's done of the book looks terrible—so I'm out here drowning my shame in MGM money for 10 weeks.

Abjectly,
Dash

The sixth novel would never come. Nick and Nora Charles still needed his attention.

AFTERWORD: A HUNDRED BUCKS

"Don't you ever think you'd like to go back to detecting once in a while just for the fun of it?"
—NORA TO NICK, IN *THE THIN MAN*

ON APRIL 1, 1935, Hammett was staying in a plush suite at his favorite Los Angeles hotel, the Beverly Wilshire, when he received a curious telegram he thought was an April Fool's hoax. It came from a Beverly Hills socialite named Lillian Ehrman, who was giving a Hollywood party that night honoring the visiting writer Gertrude Stein. Despite a guest list that already included Charlie Chaplin, Paulette Goddard, and a number of Hollywood producers, Stein especially wanted to meet Hammett, whom she admired as the master of the modern detective story.

Stein's affection for detective novels was well known to friends. "I never try to guess who has done the crime," she wrote, ". . . but I like somebody being dead and how it moves along and Dashiell Hammett was all that and more."[1] Months into a well-publicized homecoming lecture tour of America,

Stein's interest in crime had already led her to spend a rainy night touring Chicago in the back of a squad car, searching for homicides with her companion, Alice B. Toklas. She had been disappointed when the only killing her police guides could turn up nearby was "a family affair," she noted, and so was "not interesting."

Despite his first suspicions about the Ehrmans' party, Hammett decided to attend. Gertrude Stein looked, according to one columnist that spring, like Queen Victoria, but with gray, mannish hair. She was listening to Charlie Chaplin hold forth on the use of rhythm in film before she turned to ask Hammett about something she found historically "puzzling." In the nineteenth century, she argued, men wrote very inventively about all varieties of men, while female novelists largely "made the women be themselves seen splendidly or sadly or beautifully or despairingly." She continued: "Now in the twentieth century it is the men who do it . . . [T]hey are always themselves as strong or weak or mysterious or passionate or drunk or controlled but always themselves as the women used to do in the nineteenth century. Now you yourself always do it now why is it."[2]

According to Stein, who remembered things in her own rhythms, Hammett agreed with her observation and told her the answer was that nineteenth-century men had been confident, and the women were not, but twentieth-century men "have no confidence and so they have to make themselves as you say more beautiful more intriguing more everything and they cannot make any other man because they have to hold on to themselves not having any confidence."[3] In fact, having posed for the cover of his latest novel, Hammett fleshed out Stein's point quite well.

That spring night, he told Stein he was working on a new novel about fathers and sons. But he would not finish it or the many others he announced—as if to force himself to focus on his growing struggle at the typewriter—to friends, drinking partners, family, and gossip columnists over the coming years. The book projects had titles such as "There Was a Young Man," "My Brother Felix," "Toward Z," "The Valley Sheep Are Fatter," "December 1," "The Hunting Boy," and "Tulip," the last a twelve-thousand-word autobiographical fragment told by a tubercular old writer who is blocked.[4]

He was often cheered by the hope of new projects, "the pre-writing period when all is grand and vast and majestic."[5] But more and more in the 1930s, he retreated to Hollywood, which he knew would be crowded with many other distractions—all of them more pleasurable than sitting in a room trying to write novels. Writing movie dialogue at least still came easily to him, and paid quite well. "Yellow fellow that I am," he wrote Alfred Knopf after one of his escapes west, in June 1935. "I turned tail before the difficulties the new book was presenting and scurried back here to comparative ease and safety." But even if he had never written another line, what he had achieved with the stories and five published novels had unleashed a generation of crime writers, and with the third adaptation of *The Maltese Falcon*, John Huston's faithful movie version starring Humphrey Bogart as Spade in 1941, would inspire the hard-edged, fatalistic cinema style the French named "film noir." Scores of later radio and TV detectives were streetwise echoes of the Op Hammett had created during Prohibition.

One of those writers who followed him out of the pulps was the novelist Raymond Chandler, for whom Hammett had "made the detective story fun to write, not an exhausting concatenation of insignificant clues." Chandler may have met him only once, at a photographed West Coast gathering of *Black Mask* contributors in January 1936, but in 1944, in the *Atlantic Monthly*, Chandler wrote the most famous and eloquent tribute to Hammett ever published, a passionate brief for the accomplishments of the realist crime school, "The Simple Art of Murder."

Chandler saw Hammett as part of a larger triumph of the American language, a "revolutionary debunking of both the language and material of fiction" that had its roots as far back as Walt Whitman. Hammett, though, had "applied it to the detective story, and this, because of its heavy crust of English gentility and American pseudogentility, was pretty hard to get moving." Once he got it moving, however, Hammett moved murder out of the drawing room and into the alley and "gave murder back to the kind of people that commit it for reasons, not just to provide a corpse; and with the means at hand, not hand-wrought dueling pistols, curare and tropical fish." While accomplishing this, "he did over and over again what only the best writers can ever do at all. He wrote scenes that seemed never to have been written before."

Chandler concluded that while Hammett "did not wreck the formal detective story," he showed that "the detective story can be important writing. *The Maltese Falcon* may or may not be a work of genius, but an art which is capable of it is not 'by hypothesis' incapable of anything. Once a detective story can be as good as this, only the pedants will deny that it *could* be even better."[6] Chandler set his Philip Marlowe novels all over Los Angeles and had written quite successfully for Hollywood by 1944, yet apparently he never encountered Hammett again after their one recorded meeting. A casual reader of his *Atlantic* essay might be pardoned for assuming that the writer Chandler was lionizing was dead.

★　★　★

ONE NIGHT IN the thirties, Hammett was eating dinner with Lillian Hellman at the Brown Derby, on Wilshire Boulevard. It was a place he liked for its convenience to his favorite hotel across the street, and was dependably filled with movie people seated beneath rows of charcoal drawings of Hollywood stars. On the night Hellman remembered, a neighborhood figure known to locals as the Indian pushed through the Brown Derby's revolving door to sell his postcards, evaded the maître d', and worked his way through the maze of booths to stop beside Hammett's. He launched into his familiar noble pitch: "My grandfather was chief of the Sioux, my great-grandfather was killed by—"

"How much do you want?' Hammett demanded.

"Nothing from you," Hellman recalled the Indian's reply. "You told me you once arrested an Indian for murder." When Hammett opened his wallet, the Indian reached in to claim five twenties, but insisted, "I take it as a loan. You are better than most, but you—"

"Arrested an Indian for murder. That's right."

When the man had gone, after kissing Hellman's hand, she noted aloud how proud he had been to insist on a loan of the money rather than a gift. "No," Hammett corrected her. "He's a Negro pretending to be an Indian. He's a no-good stinker." When Hellman asked why, then, had he given him one hundred dollars, Hammett answered, "Because no-good stinkers get hungry too."[7]

He had come a long way from shadowing on Baltimore street corners to this room of banquettes filled with press agents, starlets, producers, and knights of the keyboard in Beverly Hills. But it was probably nice to have a stranger remind him once in a while that he used to be a detective, and a pretty good one at that. *There's Dashiell Hammett. He once arrested an Indian for murder.* That was worth a hundred bucks at least.

ACKNOWLEDGMENTS

This project began for the best of reasons: I wanted to read a book that did not exist on Dashiell Hammett's years as a real detective, and about exactly how he had made his famous transformation from Pinkerton operative to master of the American detective story. No such work existed devoted to this hazy but important period in his life, but many of the experienced Hammett chasers helped me attempt it. Mike Humbert posted my original call for materials on his superb website on Dashiell Hammett (http://www.mikehumbert.com/Dashiell_Hammett_01_Short_Bio.html), which helped get things going. My fellow writer and Hammett fan Mike Rogers then made introductions to Rick Layman, Hammett's biographer, who assured me that to understand how a man could actually go from Pinkerton op to world-beating writer, I needed to reread Hammett's stories in the order he wrote them. Layman was right. Over the decades since his 1981 landmark life *Shadow Man*, Layman has continued to produce books that deepen people's readings of the novels and stories, and with Hammett's granddaughter Julie M. Rivett, he has edited Hammett's letters and brought out collections of his screenplays and unpublished stories that challenge the limited view of Hammett left us by Lillian Hellman.

Julie Rivett was also patient with my occasional odd questions, starting with my first, highly specific query: which of Hammett's hands bore the famous imbedded knifepoint? (The exact location was never specified in the biographies.) Julie relayed the question to her mother, Hammett's younger daughter, Jo, author of *Hammett: A Daughter Remembers*. When Jo answered that she was pretty certain the knifepoint had been on his left hand, the confirmation brought the scar out of the realm of legend for me, as if she had pulled a smoke ring from the air.

A number of Hammett experts I met through the generosity of Don Herron, who is best known as the Fedora'd host of the long-running Dashiell Hammett Tour, but whose lively blog, *Up and Down These Mean Streets*, functions as a kind of hot-stove league for Hammett fans, featuring occasional guest lecturers such as the literary researcher Terry Zobeck. In 2012, Terry typed Hammett's name into a Brooklyn historical search engine called Fultonhistory.com, which surprised him by hiccupping up a long-forgotten interview Hammett did with the *Brooklyn Daily Eagle Magazine* in October 1929, just after he had moved to New York. This interview was unknown to recent biographers, and I have made generous use of it here.

Don Herron took me around San Francisco, even got me into the 891 Post Street studio where *The Maltese Falcon* was written, and shared his network of similarly helpful Hammett fans, including Bill Arney, who described his experience living with the spirit of Hammett's novel in the *Maltese Falcon* apartment; and Mitch Soekland, who gave me the tour on behalf of its gracious current renter, the writer Robert Mailer Anderson. Vince Emery, who has devoted an entire publishing company to the study and enjoyment of Hammett (Vince Emery Productions/Ace Performer Collection) gave me some helpful advice on researching tuberculosis in Hammett's time and information on his op career in general.

I am extremely grateful to the San Francisco detective and Hammett scholar David Fechheimer for his continuing insights into his elusive hero, and for his original interviews, which have proved so essential to anyone's idea of Hammett. The Hammett medical file, now missing from every possible branch of the Veterans' Administration, was fortunately copied by Fechheimer in the summer of 1976, after he was loaned it by a contact who brought it to dinner one night. Fechheimer read the whole filched document into his tape recorder, and then, after abandoning plans for his own Hammett book, sent the tape and transcript off to Richard Layman, who graciously shared it with me. So much that appears in each Hammett biography of the last four decades comes from the sleuthing of Fechheimer published in the Hammett-themed November 4, 1975 issue of Francis Ford Coppola's *City of San Francisco* magazine. I hope that if he ever retires from detecting, Fechheimer will finally write his own book.

My friend Allen Barra, a writer whose deep pockets of expertise run from gunslingers and gangsters to Alabama football and Albert Camus, is also a longtime Hammett man, and supplied his short, helpful history of the various film incarnations of *Red Harvest*—from *Roadhouse Nights* to *The Good, the Bad and the Ugly*; *Miller's Crossing* (which splits the difference between *Red Harvest* and *The Glass Key*); and *Deadwood*.

This project had many pleasures, chiefly the reading of the books themselves and touring Hammett's San Francisco, but also my time spent at the Pinkerton archive of the Library of Congress in Washington, where for days at a time I was happily surrounded by boxes of detecting paraphernalia: crumbling codebooks, posters for missing outlaws, and op reports of nineteenth-century violence captured in disconcertingly beautiful script.

Ellen Crain, archives director at the handsome Butte–Silver Bow Public Archives, was expertly helpful with research about the Frank Little killing, local miner history, and Hammett's possible experiences in that fascinating town. The people at Second Edition Books in Butte were also helpful, and patient with my questions; they recommended a few useful works of Montana history. Laura Wellen and Paul A. Gansky assisted with my research queries at the Harry Ransom archives at the University of Texas, Austin. New York University's Bobst Library offered its microfilmed collection of newspapers and some old detectives' books in its Special Collections department, while the Brooklyn Historical Society luckily had a copy of the family history of the Dashiells.

Dashiell Hammett seemed to lay around our house like a visiting uncle during the last few years, and it is no small tribute to my wonderful kids how they cheerfully carried on despite the heaps of books my worldly guest left about the place, only occasionally asking how much longer he would be with us. I thank my children, Nick and Nina, for their support, and I am ever grateful to my wife, Katie Calhoun, for her love and patience and for bringing me into her family, the Calhouns, who introduced me to Montana. Katie's oldest sister, Patty Calhoun, ambassador to all things Western, also deserves special thanks for several Hammett-related excursions we made to Butte and Anaconda.

This book started with a lunch that my agent and friend Ed Breslin arranged with George Gibson, publisher at Bloomsbury USA. George immediately saw the potential in the idea of a Hammett-as-detective book, and the proposal followed from the lunch group's excited discussion. My profound thanks go to these two literary men for the book's civilized beginnings, and to George for his patience, sharp edits, and enthusiastic counsel as it took shape.

NOTES

Prelude: SCARS

1   Dashiell Hammett, *Selected Letters of Dashiell Hammett, 1921–1960*, ed. Richard Layman and Julie Rivett (Berkeley, CA: Counterpoint, 2001), p. 146.

2   Jo Hammett, *Dashiell Hammett: A Daughter Remembers*, ed. Richard Layman and Julie Rivett (New York: Carroll and Graf, 2001), p. 74. If there is a wiser, more beautiful book on Hammett than this one by his daughter Jo, I have not found it.

3   David Fechheimer, "Dashiell Hammett's San Francisco," special issue of *City of San Francisco*, vol. 9, no. 17, Nov. 4, 1975, p. 38.

4   James H. S. Moynahan, "Dashiell Hammett Confesses!" 1934, reproduced in Richard Layman, ed., *Discovering the Maltese Falcon and Sam Spade* (San Francisco, CA: Vince Emery Productions, 2005), p. 60.

5   Dashiell Hammett, *Lost Stories*, ed. Vince Emery (Vince Emery Productions, 2005), p. 79.

6   Hammett, *Selected Letters*, p. 24.

7   "Suggestions to Detective Story Writers," in Dashiell Hammett, *Hammett: Crime Stories and Other Writings* (New York: Library of America, 2001), p. 914.

8   Dashiell Hammett, "The Scorched Face," in Hammett, *Crime Stories and Other Writings*, p. 356.

9   Dashiell Hammett, introduction to *The Maltese Falcon* (New York: Modern Library, 1934), pp. viii–ix.

10   Dashiell Hammett, *The Maltese Falcon* (New York: Vintage, 1930), p. 4.

11   Pinkerton's National Detective Agency Records, 1853–1999 (hereafter cited as Pinkerton records), Box 178, Folder 9, Manuscript Division, Library of Congress, Washington, D.C.

12   "House Burglary Poor Trade," Hammett interview with Helen Herbert Foster in *Brooklyn Daily Eagle*, Oct. 6 1929, p. 94, found on Fultonhistory.com.

13   David Fechheimer, "Mrs. Hammett is Alive and Well in L.A.," special issue of *City of San Francisco* magazine, vol. 9, no. 17, Nov. 4, 1975, p. 38.

Chapter One

1   The detective Josiah Thompson interviewed Yowaiski on David Fechheimer's behalf in August 1977. Richard Hammett was a widower by the 1930s, but it's hard to believe he had changed radically from the man Sam Hammett grew up with. The interview (in the form of an operative's report) is reproduced in Thompson's book *Gumshoe* (New York: Fawcett, 1988).

2   Hammett's 1924 biographical statement reproduced in Layman, ed., *Discovering the Maltese Falcon*, p. 12.

3   "House Burglary Poor Trade," p. 94.

4   Morris Friedman, *The Pinkerton Labor Spy* (New York: Wilshire Book Company, 1907), p. 11.

5   Ibid., p. 5.

6   Dashiell Hammett, "Zigzags of Treachery," in Hammett, *Crime Stories & Other Writings*, p. 92.

7   Charlie Siringo, *A Cowboy Detective* (Chicago: W. B. Conkey Company, 1912).

8   Allan Pinkerton, *Thirty Years a Detective* (Warwick, NY: 1500 Books, 2007), pp. 12–13.

9   James MacKay, *Allan Pinkerton: The First Private Eye* (New York: John Wiley and Sons, 1996), p. 59.

10   Pinkerton, *Thirty Years a Detective*, p. 12.

11   Allan Pinkerton, *The Model Town and the Detectives* (New York: G. W. Dillingham, 1890), preface.

12   T. J. Stiles, *Jesse James: Last Rebel of the Civil War*, (New York: Vintage, 2005), p. 257.

13   Ibid.

14   Charles A. Siringo, *Two Evil Isms: Pinkertonism and Anarchism* (Chicago, IL: C. A. Siringo, 1915), p. 105, Box 172, available at Library of Congress, Washington, D.C. "I had started out with the big agency to see the world and learn human nature," p. 93.

15   "House Burglary Poor Trade."

Chapter Two

1   Allan Pinkerton, *The Expressman and the Detectives* Chicago: W. B. Keen, Cooke and Company, 1874), p. 26.

2   March 1, 1924, in Hammett, *Selected Letters*, pp. 24–25.

3   Pinkerton records, Box 51, Folder 8.

4   Pinkerton records, Box 51, Folder 11.

5   Pinkerton records, Box 51, Folder 8.

6   After completing his own comprehensive life of Hammett, *Shadow Man* (New York: Harvest/Harcourt Brace Jovanovich, 1981), Richard Layman continued to post queries in search of proof of Jimmy Wright, whose existence still seemed probable when he wrote his biography. All other major biographies accept the existence of Wright.

7   Memo of April 20, 1901, Pinkerton records, Box 178, Folder 9.

8   Pinkerton records, Box 15, Folder 10.

9   C.Y.R. report, Aug. 7, 1910, Pinkerton records. The brakeman's quote "I can see it in my mind's eye . . ." comes from an unsigned report in Box 157, Folder 10.

10   J. V. O'Neill report, Pinkerton records, Box 157, Folder 9.

11   C. B. Patterson report, Pinkerton records, Box 157. Folder 8.

12   In reports from the investigation, the missing Sciarrabas are called cousins, and at other times, father and son. Their having the same name, Vincenzo Sciarraba, would seem odd for brothers. In this letter from 1951 (Pinkerton records, Box 87), the discrepancy is more likely a matter of an old man remembering a very old case about suspects he'd never met. See also "The Ambush of William Rice," Cleveland *Plain Dealer*, Sunday, May 4, 1941.

13   Hammett interview, *Brooklyn Daily Eagle*, Oct. 6, 1929.

Chapter Three

1   Michael Punke, *Fire and Brimstone: The North Butte Mining Disaster of 1917* (New York: Hyperion, 2006). Punke's fine narrative of the disaster cites 163 miner deaths, while briefer accounts often give 168.

2   "I.W.W. Strike Chief Lynched at Butte," *New York Times*, Aug. 1, 1917; and Will Roscoe, "The Murder of Frank Little: An Injury to One Is an Injury to All," thesis paper, Sentinel High School, Missoula, MN, 1973. Will Roscoe's paper remains the most extensive popular account of the Little incident. He also recalled researching the Little incident in a 2006 story for the Montana *Standard*.

3   Punke, *Fire and Brimstone*, p. 209. See also Montana Troopers' website, http://www.montanatrooper.com.

4   Lillian Hellman, *Scoundrel Time* (New York: Bantam, 1976), p. 46.

5   Ibid.

6   Jo Hammett, *A Daughter Remembers*, p. 34. One of Jo Hammett's collaborators going through these photos was the Hammett historian Don Herron.

7   Dashiell Hammett, *Red Harvest* (New York: Vintage, 1929), pp. 3–4.

Chapter Four

1   "World War I: The Ambulance Service," U.S. Army Medical Department, Office of Medical History, chapter 2, section 40 at http://history.amedd.army.mil/booksdocs/HistoryofUSArmyMSC/chapter2.html.

2   John M. Barry, *The Great Influenza: The Story of the Deadliest Pandemic in History* (New York: Penguin, 2004), p. 239. Also see the short Stanford University publication by Molly Billings, "The Influenza Pandemic of 1918," June 1997, at https://virus.stanford.edu/uda/.

3   Barry, *The Great Influenza*, p. 187.

4   Hammett's initial diagnosis details are from a transcript of his Veterans' Administration medical file, transcribed by David Fechheimer on June 17, 1976, and provided to me by Richard Layman (hereafter cited as Hammett VA medical file), pp. 1–3. The VA itself was unable to locate an existing copy in its St. Louis (national records), San Francisco, or Oakland facilities.

5   Hammett's VA medical file.

6   Author's correspondence with the New York pulmonary specialist Dr. Brian D. Gelbman, March 3, 2013. I shared with Dr. Gelbman the initial diagnosis from Hammett's VA medical file, and described the close-packed hospital setting in which he was cared for during the influenza outbreak. He agreed it was more likely Hammett had contracted TB while in hospital, weakened initially by the influenza. The army doctors at the time agreed. Of course, with as many specialists as Hammett saw over the years, his file seems more expert some years than in others.

7   Jo Hammett, *Hammett: A Daughter Remembers*, p. 72.

8   "From the Memoirs of a Private Detective," collected in *Hammett: Crime Stories & Other Writings*, p. 909.

9   All discussions of Hammett's weight and other medical details come from Hammett's V.A. medical file.

Chapter Five

1   The twelve surviving love letters, the so-called green-ink letters, turned up in "an old pasteboard hatbox, faded and dusty," Julie Rivett has written, while the family was cleaning out the last of her late grandmother Jose Hammett's things before the house was sold. ("On Finding My Grandfather's Love Letters," by Julie Marshall Rivett, which was e-mailed to the author.) The letters appear in Hammett, *Selected Letters*. I have supplemented the letters and accounts of the romance in the Layman, Johnson, and Symons biographies with other background histories of World War I nursing.

2   Hammett, *Selected Letters*, p. 10.

3   Ibid., p. 20.

Chapter Six

1   "Tuberculosis Victims to be Rehabilitated," *San Francisco Chronicle*, July 2, 1922.

2   Oakland *Tribune*, March 4, 1922, and *San Francisco Chronicle*, March 6, 1922. This last incident sounds some notes echoed in Hammett's story "Dead Yellow Women," in *Dead Yellow Women* (New York: Lawrence E. Spivak, 1924).

3   Hammett's VA medical file.

4   Author's lunch with Fechheimer, July 12, 2012. We have had a couple of lunches together in San Francisco, and he has been a generous e-mail correspondent as well about Hammett arcana and, equally important to a civilian writer, the detective life in general.

5   Fechheimer, "We Never Sleep: The Old Pinkertons Look Back," interview with Phil Haultain, in *City of San Francisco* magazine, vol. 9, no. 17, Nov. 4, 1975. p. 33.

6   Dashiell Hammett, "Seven Pages," in *The Hunter and Other Stories* (New York: Mysterious Press, 2013), p. 142.

7   Introduction to Dashiell Hammett, *The Big Knockover* (New York: Vintage, 1989), p. xiii.

8   David Fechheimer, "We Never Sleep: The Old Pinkertons Look Back," interview with Phil Haultain, in *City of San Francisco* magazine, vol. 9, no. 17, Nov. 4, 1975, p.33.

9   I compiled this account of the cable car robbery and its aftermath using mainly contemporary newspaper accounts. On January 4, 1922, the *San Francisco Chronicle* ran a full map of the thieves' route, complete with photo insets of the company officials and the gripman and conductor, "Victims of Daylight Robbery on Street Car." Phil Geauque appears in the January 9 *Chronicle* follow-up, "Sleuths Shoot at Cable Car Bandit Suspect." Haultain's comments are from Fechheimer's interview with him, "We Never Sleep . . ." in *City of San Francisco* magazine, vol. 9, no. 17, Nov. 4, 1975.

10   Hammett's VA medical file.

11   David Fechheimer, "Mrs. Hammett is Alive and Well in L.A." *City of San Francisco* magazine, vol. 9, no. 17, Nov. 4, 1975, p. 36.

Chapter Seven

1   William Pinkerton came to San Francisco whenever he could, often for the convention of police chiefs. My

portrait of him draws from several long interviews he happily gave to the *Chronicle* in the teens and early twenties (including "Pinkerton Here to Curb Crooks," Feb. 8, 1915; and "Fiction Wrong about Sleuths, Moving Pictures Mirror Them Truthfully, Says Pinkerton," June 21, 1922), and from book-length histories of the Pinkerton organization (*Allan Pinkerton: The First Private Eye*, by James MacKay; *The Eye That Never Sleeps*, by Frank Morn; and *Pinkerton's Great Detective*, by Beau Riffenburgh).

2 "Fiction Wrong about Sleuths," p. 16.

3 It is interesting to picture him as a reporter, especially in that combative time of muckraking journalism, which might have appealed to his antiauthority bent and confirmed his violent experiences with corruption.

4 The William Sayers story appears in "Pinkerton Man Retires: Superintendent Sayers Goes South for His Health," *San Francisco Chronicle*, Oct. 22, 1902. William Pinkerton's forger tale is told in "Forger Bidwell: Detective Pinkerton's Story of his Crime and Arrest," *Minneapolis Tribune*, picked up by the *San Francisco Chronicle*, Sept. 27, 1887.

5 Carroll John Daly, "Knights of the Open Palm," from Otto Penzler, ed., *The Black Lizard Big Book of* Black Mask *Stories* (New York: Vintage Crime/Black Lizard, 2010), p. 429.

6 Hammett, *Dead Yellow Women*, pp. 94–95.

7 Hammett, *Dead Yellow Women*, p. 95.

8 "House Burglary Poor Trade." He started with a nameless "type" and "just kept going," he wrote his *Black Mask* editor.

9   Hammett, *Selected Letters*, p. 22. Berkeley's chief of police
        August Vollmer was a favorite of the Bay Area press, using
        "psychology instead of the Third Degree" and relying on
        a strange new machine to tell when suspects were lying:
        William Hamlin, "What Happens When Your Heart
        Goes Pit-a-Pat," *San Francisco Chronicle*, March 20, 1921;
        "Super Police Trail Thieves By Radio," *San Francisco
        Chronicle*, Oct. 9, 1921; "Greater Study of Crime Urged by
        Police Head," *San Francisco Chronicle*, Aug. 2, 1922.

                              Chapter Eight

1   This quote appears in the preface to J. Anthony Lukas's
        *Big Trouble: A Murder in a Small Town Sets Off a Struggle
        for the Soul of America* (New York: Simon and Schuster,
        1997), a magnificent and forgivably sprawling account
        of the 1905 murder of Idaho's former governor and
        the subsequent trial in which Clarence Darrow defended
        Haywood and the Western Federation of Miners leader-
        ship in a case made largely by the Great Detective, James
        McParland. The Pinkertons even managed to get one of
        their own, Operative 21, onto Darrow's defense team.
        Lukas's book has the best portrait of McParland and the
        Pinkertons of this time that I have read, and he alone
        suggests (as an aside) that McParland inspired Hammett's
        Old Man character. It is one of the few side roads in
        Lukas's story that he doesn't eagerly explore, on the notion
        that it will eventually wind back around to the great main
        drama he's describing. No proper Hammett biography I
        have seen has followed this thread.

2   Local newspapers in Seattle or Helena or Portland would interview McParland as a visiting celebrity when he made his occasional rounds, with story headlines such as the one a Seattle paper used in 1903: "Looking After the Criminals." When McParland's inspection tour reached Montana later the same year, a Helena paper editorialized that "[A]t his tongue's end is the history of every train and bank robber who has operated in the West from the cradle to the grave."

3   From Pinkerton records, Part A: Administrative File, 1857–1999, Reel 4, Frames 0979–0980.

4   Allan Pinkerton, *The Mollie Maguires and the Detectives* (New York: G. W. Dillingham, 1877), p. 23. But another memorable account of the Molly Maguires investigation appears in James D. Horan and Howard Swiggett's *The Pinkerton Story* (New York: Putnam, 1951). Horan seems to have been on such good terms with the agency that many of its files were kept in his house while he researched this official book, and here and there, his papers and other memos turn up among the folders in the Pinkerton records.

5   This (and many other McParland stories) appears in the recent full biography, Beau Riffenburgh, *Pinkerton's Great Detective: The Amazing Life and Times of James McParland* (New York: Viking, 2013).

Chapter Nine

1   Hammett's VA medical file.

2   Layman, *Shadow Man*, p. 58. This assumes a penny-per-word rate, which was average, and his selling two stories per month.

3   From Hammett, *Lost Stories*, p. 142.

4   Hammett, *Selected Letters*, pp. 26–27.

5   Raymond Chandler, *Trouble Is My Business* (New York: Vintage, 1992), p. 8.

6   Layman, ed., *Discovering the Maltese Falcon*, p. 75. This anecdote is from an interview that Layman had with Gardner.

Chapter Ten

1   Albert Samuels, "Just About Ourselves—Eighty of Us" (advertisement), *San Francisco Chronicle*, Dec. 3, 1922.

2   E. Sherwood, "A Jeweler Pays for Advertising Lost Articles," *Printers' Ink*, May 20, 1920, p. 137.

3   Ad reproduced in Jo Hammett, *A Daughter Remembers*, p. 51.

4   "Seven Pages" (unpublished typescript), reproduced in Layman, ed., *Discovering the Maltese Falcon*.

5   Dashiell Hammett, *The Glass Key* (New York: Vintage, 1989), p. 14.

6   Hammett, *Selected Letters*, p. 30.

7   Hammett's VA medical file.

8   I do not suggest this as the only possible inspiration, but Hammett did love to read crime news. Don Herron has nominated a film from 1920 as the genesis, *The Penalty*, starring Lon Chaney as a master criminal known as "Blizzard, the cripple from Hell," and which features a messy street battle and a heist. The idea was certainly in the air. There was a time in the early twenties, before the rise of Hammett and the *Black Mask* style of writing, when movies were more realistic than novels in their

depictions of crime. William Pinkerton commented on this in 1921, finding the cinematic crime stories startlingly accurate, almost instructively so, while detective novels remained preposterous "bunk."

Chapter Eleven

1   Hammett, *Red Harvest*, pp. 3–4.

2   The Montana historian Jack Crowley has made a good study of the similarities between Personville and Butte in his 2008 paper "*Red Harvest* and Dashiell Hammett's Butte," in *Montana Professor* 18, no. 2 (Spring 2008), at http://mtprof.msun.edu. Another good discussion can be found in George Everett's "The Seeds of *Red Harvest*: Dashiell Hammett's Poisonville" post in the blog *Only in Butte* (www.butteamerica.com/hist.htm), and Don Herron paints the strikebreaking scene well in his post, "Hammett: Playing the Sap," from his Hammett blog *Up and Down These Mean Streets* (March 5, 2011). Some reviewers have seen the novel as a muckraking work of semi-reportage like *The Jungle*. André Gide saw it as a Marxist tract.

3   Punke, *Fire and Brimstone*, p. 211. Punke does not discuss Hammett's claims, but the disgraced chief detective Morrissey seems a far likelier suspect in the Little death.

4   Hammett, *Red Harvest*, p. 86.

5   Jo Hammett, *A Daughter Remembers*, p. 62.

6   Hammett, *Red Harvest*, p. 163.

7   From an e-mail with the author, March 29, 2012.

8   Date per Layman, *Shadow Man*, p. 98. Quote about "motion picture dickering" per Diane Johnson, *Dashiell*

Hammett: A Life (New York: Fawcett/Columbine, 1983), p. 73. Julian Symons also has an excellent account of Hammett's adventures in Hollywood in *Dashiell Hammett* (New York: Harcourt Brace Jovanovich, 1985), pp. 73–81.

Chapter Twelve

1   Hammett, *Maltese Falcon*, Modern Library ed., introduction.

2   Hammett, *Maltese Falcon*, Vintage ed., p. 90.

3   Arney was quite generous with my e-mailed questions and even wrote me a definitive account of his life in the apartment, when I was unable to locate a copy of the brochure he'd once written about it. Also see the *New York Times* travel story "San Francisco Noir" (June 29, 2014), and Don Herron's blog post "Hammett and Prohibition," in *Up and Down These Mean Streets*, Dec. 25, 2014, (see "891 Post," at http://www.donherron.com/?p=7465), and in the same blog, Herron's splendid write-ups of all the Hammett apartments, covered individually in "The Tour" (at http://www.donherron.com/?page_id=51).

Chapter Thirteen

For Hammett's years in Hollywood, I consulted Diane Johnson's *Dashiell Hammett*, William Nolan's *Hammett: A Life at the Edge*, Julian Symons's Hammett biography, Lillian Hellman's books, and Layman's *Shadow Man*. But Layman's commentaries in *The Hunter* and *Return of the Thin Man* are especially useful.

1   Layman, *Shadow Man*, p. 125.

2   Hammett, *Selected Letters*, p. 50.

3   Hammett, *The Glass Key*, p. 6.

4   Layman, *Shadow Man*, p. 125.

5   Ibid.

6   Lillian Hellman, *An Unfinished Woman* (New York: Bantam, 1974), p. 226. In the account of the meeting in Diane Johnson's *Hammett: A Life*, which Johnson wrote with Hellman's active participation, someone introduced the pair at Musso and Frank, the Hollywood bar and grill on Hollywood Boulevard that's still there. Since Hammett was already known to her husband, and the two shared a group of friends, chances are they looked each other over at several gatherings before the extended night of drinking and T. S. Eliot.

7   Symons, *Dashiell Hammett*, p. 74.

8   W. E. Farbstein, "Techniques of Stopping a Run on a Bank," *New York Herald Tribune*, April 26, 1931.

9   Jo Hammet, *A Daughter Remembers*, p. 70.

10   Johnson, *Dashiell Hammett*, p. 103.

11   The story of the writing of *The Thin Man* appears in various bios and in Hellman's *Unfinished Woman*, and in *The Last Laugh: The Final Word from the First Name in Satire*, by S. J. Perleman (Guilford, CT: Lyons Press, 2000), whose account of Hammett's sneaky departure from the Pierre is unrivaled. But the most thorough account of Hammett's time at the Sutton appears in Marion Meade's *Lonelyhearts: The Screwball Life of Nathanael West and Eileen McKenney* (New York: Mariner/

Harcourt Brace Jovanovich, 2010). Meade identifies Hammett's rooms as the Diplomatic Suite.

12   Hellman, *An Unfinished Woman*, p. 270.

13   Dashiell Hammett, *The Thin Man* (1933; repr. New York: Vintage, 1972), p. 7.

14   Hammett, *Selected Letters*, p. 84.

Afterword: A HUNDRED BUCKS

1   Johnson, *Dashiell Hammett*, p. 126. For an account of the Stein party, see James B. Mellow, *Charmed Circle* (Santa Barbara, CA: Praeger, 1974), pp. 407–8.

2   Mellow, *Charmed Circle*, pp. 407–8. Alma Whitaker's *Los Angeles Times* column (Sugar & Spice) of April 2, 1935, contains the comparison to Queen Victoria and concludes, "She is either diabolically humorous or completely devoid of that trait. I'm still not sure." See also Gertrude Stein, "Why I Like Detective Stories," *Harper's Bazaar*, Nov. 1937; and Stein's own *Everybody's Autobiography* (New York: Random House, 1937), p. 193. For further evidence of Stein's appreciation of what Hammett could do, see her posthumously published attempt at a detective novel, *Blood on the Dining Room Floor*. Part of her impressions of the homecoming tour ran in the February 1935 *Cosmopolitan* magazine.

3   Johnson, *Dashiell Hammett*, p. 126.

4   These titles are assembled from a number of interviews and letters over the years, one of them given quickly to a *Los Angeles Times* reporter who found Hammett on his way to visit his daughter in LA.

5   Hammett, *Selected Letters*, p. 417.

6   Raymond Chandler, *The Simple Art of Murder* (New York: Vintage Crime, 1988), p. 15.

7   Hellman, *An Unfinished Woman*, p. 54.

SELECTED BIBLIOGRAPHY

BOOKS

Asbury, Herbert. *The Barbary Coast: An Informal History of the San Francisco Underworld*. New York: Garden City Publishing, 1933.

Barry, John M. *The Great Influenza: The Story of the Deadliest Pandemic in History*. New York: Penguin, 2004.

Blum, Howard. *Dark Invasion. 1915: Germany's Secret War and the Hunt for the First Terrorist Cell in America*. New York: HarperCollins, 2014.

Burnett, W. R. *Little Caesar*. New York: Avon, 1945. First published 1929 by Dial Press.

Chandler, Raymond. *The Simple Art of Murder*. New York: Vintage Crime, 1988.

———. *Trouble Is My Business*. New York: Vintage Crime, 1992.

Dashiell, Benjamin Jones. *Dashiell Family Records*, Vols. 1–3. Baltimore, MD: B. H. Dashiell, 1928–1932.

Dillon, Richard H. *Hatchet Men: The Story of the Tong Wars in San Francisco's Chinatown*. Fairfield and Vacaville: JSP Pub, 1962.

Doyle, Sir Arthur Conan. *The Valley of Fear.* New York: Berkley Publishing, 1915.

Edwords, Clarence E. *Bohemian San Francisco: Its Restaurants and Their Most Famous Recipes.* San Francisco, CA: Paul Elder and Company, 1914.

Fenton, Charles A. *The Apprenticeship of Ernest Hemingway: The Early Years.* New York: Viking, 1954.

Friedman, Morris. *The Pinkerton Labor Spy.* Chatsworth, CA: Wilshire Book Co., 1907.

Glasscock, C. B. *The War of the Copper Kings.* Helena, MT: Riverbend Publications, 2002. First published 1935 by The Bobbs-Merrill Co.

Hammett, Dashiell. *The Big Knockover.* New York: Vintage Crime, 1989.

———. *Blood Money.* New York: Dell, 1947.

———. *The Continental Op.* New York: Dell, 1945.

———. *The Continental Op.* Edited by Steven Marcus. New York: Vintage, 1992.

———. *The Dain Curse.* New York: Vintage, 1989.

———. *Dashiell Hammett: Selected Letters, 1921-1960.* Edited by Richard Layman, and Julie M. Rivett. Berkeley, CA: Counterpoint, 2001.

———. *Dead Yellow Women.* New York: Laurence E. Spivak, 1947.

———. *The Glass Key.* New York: Vintage, 1989.

———. *Hammett: Crime Stories and Other Writings.* New York: Library of America, 2001.

———. *The Hunter and Other Stories.* Edited by Richard Layman and Julie M. Rivett. (New York: Mysterious Press, 2013).

———. *Lost Stories.* Edited by Vince Emery. San Francisco, CA: Vince Emery Productions, 2005.

——. *The Maltese Falcon*. New York: Vintage, 1992. First published 1930 by Alfred A. Knopf.

——. *The Maltese Falcon*. New York: Modern Library, 1934.

——. *A Man Called Spade and Other Stories*. New York: Dell, 1944.

——. *Nightmare Town: Stories*. New York: Vintage Crime, 1999.

——. *Red Harvest*. New York: Vintage Crime, 1992. First published 1929 by Alfred A. Knopf.

——. *The Return of the Continental Op*. New York: Dell, 1945.

——. *Return of the Thin Man*. Edited by Richard Layman and Julie M. Rivett. New York: Mysterious Press, 2012.

——. *The Thin Man*. New York: Vintage, 1972. First published 1933 by Alfred A. Knopf.

——. *Woman in the Dark: A Novel of Dangerous Romance*. New York: Alfred A. Knopf, 1933.

Hammett, Jo. *Dashiell Hammett: A Daughter Remembers*. Edited by Richard Layman and Julie M. Rivett. New York: Carroll and Graf, 2001.

Hellman, Lillian. *Scoundrel Time*. New York: Bantam, 1976.

——. *An Unfinished Woman*. New York: Bantam, 1974.

Herron, Don. *The Dashiell Hammett Tour*. San Francisco, CA: Emery/Ace Performer, 2009.

Holt, Patricia. *The Good Detective: True Cases from the Confidential Files of Hal Lipset, America's Real-Life Sam Spade*. New York: Pocket, 1991.

Horan, James D., and Howard Swiggett. *The Pinkerton Story*. New York: Putnam, 1951.

Johnson, Diane. *Dashiell Hammett: A Life*. New York: Fawcett Columbine, 1983.

Johnson, Paul C. *The Early Sunset Magazine, 1898–1928.* San Francisco, CA: California Historical Society, 1973.

Layman, Richard, ed. *Discovering the Maltese Falcon and Sam Spade.* San Francisco, CA: Vince Emery Productions, 2005.

——, ed. *Literary Masters Volume 3: Dashiell Hammett.* Farmington Hills, MI: Gale, 2000.

——. *Shadow Man: The Life of Dashiell Hammett.* New York: Harvest/Harcourt Brace Jovanovich, 1981.

Lukas, J. Anthony. *Big Trouble: A Murder in a Small Western Town Sets off a Struggle for the Soul of America.* New York: Simon and Schuster, 1997.

MacKay, James. *Allan Pinkerton: The First Private Eye.* New York: John Wiley and Sons, 1996.

McWatters, George S. *Knots Untied: Or, Ways and By-Ways in the Hidden Life of American Detectives.* Hartford, CT: J. B. Burr and Hyde, 1871.

Meade, Marion. *Lonelyhearts: The Screwball World of Nathanael West and Eileen McKenney.* New York: Mariner/Harcourt Brace Jovanovich, 2010.

Mellow, James B. *Charmed Circle.* Santa Barbara, CA: Praeger, 1974.

Morn, Frank. *The Eye That Never Sleeps: A History of the Pinkerton National Detective Agency.* Bloomington: Indiana University Press, 1975.

Nolan, William. *Dashiell Hammett: A Casebook.* Santa Barbara, CA: McNally and Loftin, 1969.

——. *Hammett: A Life at the Edge.* New York: Congdon and Weed, 1983.

O'Brien, Robert. *This Is San Francisco: A Classic Portrait of the*

City. San Francisco, CA: Chronicle Books, 1994. First published 1948 by Whittlesey House.

Penzler, Otto, ed. *The Black Lizard Big Book of Black Mask Stories*. New York: Vintage Crime/Black Lizard, 2010.

Perelman, S. J. *The Last Laugh: The Final Word from the First Name in Satire*. Guilford, CT: Lyons Press, 2000.

Pinkerton, Allan. *The Model Town and the Detectives*. New York: G. W. Dillingham, 1876.

———. *The Mollie Maguires and the Detectives*. G. W. Dillingham, 1877.

———. *The Expressman and the Detective*. Chicago: W. B. Keen, Cooke, 1874.

———. *Thirty Years a Detective*. Warwick, NY: 1500 Books, 2007.

Poe, Edgar Allan. *Great Short Works of Edgar Allan Poe*. New York: Perennial, 1970.

Punke, Michael. *Fire and Brimstone: The North Butte Mining Disaster of 1917*. New York: Hyperion, 2006.

Riffenburgh, Beau. *Pinkerton's Great Detective: The Amazing Life and Times of James McParland*. New York: Viking, 2013.

Rothman, Sheila. *Living in the Shadow of Death: Tuberculosis and the Social Experience of Illness in American History*. Baltimore, MD: Johns Hopkins University Press, 1994.

Stanford, Sally. *The Lady of the House*. New York: Putnam, 1966.

Stewart, Donald Ogden, ed. *Fighting Words*. Harcourt Brace, 1940.

Stiles, T. J. *Jesse James: Last Rebel of the Civil War*. New York: Vintage, 2003.

Summerscale, Kate. *The Suspicions of Mr. Whicher*. New York: Bloomsbury, 2008.

Symons, Julian. *Dashiell Hammett*. New York: Harcourt Brace Jovanovich, 1985.

Thompson, Josiah. *Gumshoe*. New York: Fawcett, 1988.

Triplett, Frank. *The Life, Times, and Treacherous Death of Jesse James*. Columbus, OH: The Swallow Press, 1970. First published 1882 by J.H. Chambers & Co., Chicago.

Vidocq, François Eugene. *Memoirs of Vidocq: Master of Crime*. Oakland, CA: AK Press/Nabat, 2003.

Wright Cobb, Sally, and Mark Willems. *The Brown Derby Restaurant*. New York: Rizzoli, 1996.

PERIODICALS

"All Sonoma Minted Gold Found; Sailor Suspected." *San Francisco Chronicle*, Dec. 2, 1921, p. 1.

"The Ambush of William Rice." (Cleveland) *Plain Dealer Sunday Magazine*, May 4, 1941.

"Boston Women Laud Finger Print Plan." *Finger Print and Identification Magazine*, 4, no. 1 (July 1922): 4.

Chandler, Raymond. "Writers in Hollywood." *The Atlantic*, Nov. 1945.

"Charges Rice Death to 'Rich Interests.'"(Cleveland) *Plain Dealer*, Jan. 12, 1911, p. 1.

Daly, John Jay. "Secrets of the Secret Service." (Uniontown, PA) *Daily News Standard*, April 5, 1939, p. 11.

"Daring Thieves Rob Woman of $3000 in Gems." *San Francisco Chronicle*, Nov. 20, 1920, p. 6.

"Dashiell Hammett Has Hard Words for Tough Stuff He Used to Write." *Los Angeles Times*, June 7, 1950, p. A3.

"Deed Executed with Finger Prints." Editorial. *Finger Print and Identification Magazine* 2, no. 4 (Oct. 1920): 2.

"Ex-Pastor, Held as Thief, Admits Many Burglaries." *San Francisco Chronicle*, Jan. 13, 1922, p. 1.

Farbstein W. E. "Technique of Stopping a Run on a Bank." *New York Herald Tribune*, April 26, 1931, p. 10.

Fechheimer, David. "Dashiell Hammett's San Francisco." Special issue *City of San Francisco* magazine 9, no. 17, Nov. 4, 1975.

"Fiction Wrong about Sleuths, Moving Pictures Mirror Them Truthfully, Says Pinkerton." *San Francisco Chronicle*, June 21, 1922, p. 16.

"Greater Study of Crime Urged by Police Head." *San Francisco Chronicle*, Aug. 2, 1922, p. 11.

Hammett, Dashiell. "Albert Pastor at Home." *Esquire: The Quarterly for Men.* Autumn 1933, p. 34.

"Hammett Will Do Stage Play." *Los Angeles Times*, May 29, 1934, p. 10.

"Have Sworn to Destroy the Rulers of China." *San Francisco Call* 83, no. 40 (Jan. 9, 1898): 1. The *Call's* reporter goes undercover into the Tong gangs of San Francisco.

"The Issue in Butte." *The New Republic*, Sept. 22, 1917, pp. 215–16.

The Jewelers' Circular 83, no. 2 (Nov. 16, 1921). For quote from Phil Geauque about jewel thief, p. 121.

Lieber, Fritz. "Stalking Sam Spade." *California Living*, Jan. 13, 1974.

"Oakland Captive Found Guilty of St. Paul Robbery." *San Francisco Chronicle*, June 25, 1922, p. B1.

"Oakland Police Arrest Two in $130,000 Theft." *San Francisco Chronicle*, March 11, 1922, p. 13.

"$104,000 Sonoma Gold Recovered; Three Held." *San Francisco Chronicle*, Nov. 29, 1921, p. 1.

Pierpont, Claudia Roth. "Tough Guy: The Mystery of Dashiell Hammett." *New Yorker*, Feb. 11, 2002, pp. 66–75.

"Pinkerton Here to Curb Crooks." *San Francisco Chronicle*, Feb. 8, 1915, p. 12.

"Pinkerton Man Retires." *San Francisco Chronicle*, Oct. 22, 1902, p. 14.

"Pinkerton Men Finish Work on Liquor Robbery." *San Francisco Chronicle*, March 6, 1922, p. 2.

"Pinkertons Claim Rice Case Solved." (Cleveland) *Plain Dealer*, Feb. 15, 1912, p. 1.

"Quartet Holds Up Officials on Cable Car." *San Francisco Chronicle*, Jan. 4, 1922, p. 1.

Rivett, Julie M. "On Samuel Spade and Samuel Dashiell Hammett: A Granddaughter's Perspective." *Clues: A Journal of Detection* 23, no. 2 (Winter 2005): 11–20.

Roberts, Charles. "The Cushman Indian Trades School and World War I." *American Indian Quarterly* 11, no. 3 (Summer 1987): 221–39.

Saltzstein, Dan. "San Francisco Noir." *New York Times*, June 6, 2014, Travel section, p. 1.

Scheuer, Philip K. "Career as Detective Gives Mystery Writer No 'Ideas.'" *Los Angeles Times*, Nov. 11, 1934, p. A3.

"S.F. Cable Car Bandit Suspect Under Arrest." *San Francisco Chronicle*, Jan. 8, 1922, p. B11.

Sherwood, E. "A Jeweler Pays for Advertising Lost Articles." *Printer's Ink* 111 (May 20, 1920): p.137.

"Sleuths Begin Man Hunt for Members of Menlo Park Crew of Bandits." *San Francisco Chronicle*, March 3, 1922, p. 3.

"Sleuths Shoot at Cable Car Bandit Suspect." *San Francisco Chronicle*, Jan. 9, 1922, p. 3.

Stein, Gertrude. "Why I Like Detective Stories." *Harper's Bazaar*, Nov. 1937.

"Stolen Gold Removed Here, Say Officials." *San Francisco Chronicle*, Nov. 26, 1921, p. 3.

"Super Police Trail Thieves by Radio." *San Francisco Chronicle*, Oct. 9, 1921, p. E1.

"Suspected Murderer from East Captured." *San Francisco Chronicle*, Feb. 22, 1911, p. 12.

"Swindler Uses Novel Plan to Escape Police." *San Francisco Chronicle*, March 29, 1921, p. 11.

Trobits, Monika. "Dashiell Hammett's San Francisco in the 1920s." *The Argonaut: Journal of the San Francisco Museum and Historical Society* (Winter 2011): 36.

"Tuberculosis Victims to be Rehabilitated." *San Francisco Chronicle*, July 2, 1922, p. F4.

"Victims of Daylight Robbery on Street Car." *San Francisco Chronicle*, Jan. 4, 1922, p. 2.

"Warrant for Quartermaster Of Sonoma Issued in Theft of $122,000 Gold on Liner." *San Francisco Chronicle*, Dec. 3, 1921, p. 3.

Watts, Richard Jr. "A Defense of Gangster Films." *New York Herald Tribune*, April 26, 1931, p. 4.

ARCHIVES

Butte–Silver Bow Public Archives.

Brooklyn Historical Society/Othmer Library.

Harry Ransom Center/University of Texas at Austin.

Homestead (FL) Historic Town Hall Museum.

New York City Municipal Archives.

New York Public Library (Forty-Second Street branch).

New York University/Bobst Library.

Pinkerton's National Detective Agency Records, 1853–1999, Manuscript Division, Library of Congress, Washington, D.C.

San Francisco History Center/San Francisco Public Library (main branch).

WEBSITES AND BLOGS

Ancestry (www.ancestry.com)

For census and military records, including Hammett's draft registration, and family tree. See where he lived when and what he was calling himself.

The Dashiell Hammett Website (www.mikehumbert.com)

An excellent gathering place for Hammett fans, with photo galleries, Hammett news, and a publishing chronology that is as helpful as it is beautiful.

Detnovel (www.DetNovel.com)

A good background resource for short bios and novel encapsulations.

January Magazine (januarymagazine.com)

See Richard Layman, "There's Only One Maltese Falcon," Feb. 15, 2005.

Montana Professor: A Journal of Education, Politics, and Culture (http://mtprof.msun.edu)

See Jack Crowley, "*Red Harvest* and Dashiell Hammett's Butte," *The Montana Professor* 18, no. 2 (Spring 2008).

Only in Butte (www.butteamerica.com/hist.htm)

See George Everett's "The Seeds of *Red Harvest*: Dashiell Hammett's Poisonville."

San Francisco City Directories Online (http://sfpl.org/index. php?pg=2000540401)

The History Center at the San Francisco Public Library also has many of its holdings online, such as city directories over the years, helpful for tracking Hammett's moves around his adopted town.

SFGate (www.SFGate.com)

See Marianne Constantinou, "This Aspiring Poet Read *The Maltese Falcon* and His Life was Transformed," Feb. 15, 2005.

SFWeekly (www.SFWeekly.com)

See "Best Private Investigator," May 11, 2011.

Smithsonian (www.smithsonian.com)

See Megan Gambino, "When Gertrude Stein Toured America," Oct. 14, 2011; also Gilbert King, "The Skinny on the Fatty Arbuckle Trial," Nov. 8, 2011.

Strand Magazine (www.StrandMag.com)

A serious and lush revival publication devoted largely to Sherlock Holmes, but which made news recently with several "lost" Hammett stories. Also features interviews with current mystery authors and excerpts from new works.

Thrilling Detective (http://www.thrillingdetective.com)

Among its hard-boiled offerings, this site ran the now-famous photograph of the gathering of West Coast *Black Mask* contributors at which Chandler and Hammett met.

Up and Down These Mean Streets (www.donherron.com)

In Don Herron's blog, "Hammett: Playing the Sap" March 5, 2011, and so many other entries on this vital Hammett site run by the town crier of the hard-boiled world and founder of the city's famous Hammett tour. All things Hammett eventually go through Don's website, hopefully with his commentary.

Up from the Deep (http://upfromthedeep.com)
Especially strong for its architectural survey of the historical Tenderloin.

The Virtual Museum of the City of San Francisco (http://www.sfmuseum.org)
A research site for scholars and buffs or families researching their San Francisco history. It offers terrific slide shows as well as its Register of the 1906 dead in the earthquake and fire.

Weekly Standard (www.WeeklyStandard.com)
See Lauren Weiner, "The Bull of Baltimore," Nov. 10, 2010.

INDEX

ABOUT THE AUTHOR

Nathan Ward is the author of *Dark Harbor: The War for the New York Waterfront*. He was an editor at *American Heritage*, and he has written for the *New York Times*, the *Wall Street Journal*, and other publications. He lives in Brooklyn, New York.